PRAISE FOR

JESUS UNEXPECTED

"One of the most difficult aspects of my own faith journey was the slow (ten years) and painfully arduous work of walking away from the Dispensational, *Left Behind* end-times views in which I was raised. [In *Jesus Unexpected*,] Keith Giles has crafted a deeply helpful and valuable gift that would have saved me years. As you read, question everything, be open and ask the Holy Spirit to teach you."

— WM. PAUL YOUNG, AUTHOR OF *THE SHACK*

"Keith Giles' *Jesus Unexpected* is a welcome addition to his helpfully provocative series. As usual, he saturates his arguments with scriptural investigation, this time emphasizing the ways in which Christ has already 'come again.'

His takedown of Dispensational misapprehensions is medicine for those of us who experienced the agony of *Left Behind* trauma, meeting and refuting that popular, colossal mistake on its own terms. His preterist read of the Olivet Discourse and the book of Revelation is careful and convincing. But what I most appreciated was that Giles was able to walk us out of our lust for mechanical certitude and into a humble (and ancient) recognition of the Mystery of Resurrection, rather than repeating the modern hubris of eschatological presumption. Nicely done."

— BRAD JERSAK, DEAN OF THEOLOGY & CULTURE, ST. STEPHEN'S UNIVERSITY (NB, CANADA), AUTHOR OF *IN: INCARNATION & INCLUSION, ABBA & LAMB*

"Though most evangelicals don't realize it, the Dispensational understanding of 'the end times' that most contemporary evangelicals espouse—including the belief in 'the rapture,' 'the Tribulation,' and the ultimate restoration of Israel—is a very recent theological innovation. Moreover, as Keith demonstrates throughout *Jesus Unexpected,* it's a theological innovation that is rooted in a seriously distorted reading of Scripture and that has harmed a lot of people and that continues to seriously hinder the credibility of the Gospel. Sticking close to Scripture at every point, Keith masterfully exposes the errors of Dispensational Theology while offering readers an alternative preterist interpretation of the New Testament's eschatology that liberates readers from fear and that calls on them to participate in what God is doing *now* to reconcile all things to himself. Anyone who cares what the New Testament says about 'the end times' owes it to themselves to read this insightful work."

— GREG BOYD, AUTHOR OF *THE MYTH OF A CHRISTIAN NATION*

"What we foresee for the future can energize us or paralyze us. One of the most paralyzing visions of the future is one that has captured modern imagination with addictive fear, and is supported by a secret code in a holy text, understood only by a select few. Dispensationalism is a world view that has kept many

Christians blind to the beauty that is present, keeping them pre-occupied with dread about the horror to come. Nothing frees us from this irrational fear as effectively as a clear understanding of how and where these twisted ideas were developed. In *Jesus Unexpected*, Keith Giles not only does that, but also draws our attention to something more captivatingly beautiful—the presence of Christ within us inviting us to participate in an adventure that is already happening."

— ANDRE RABE, AUTHOR, PUBLIC SPEAKER, PHILOSOPHER, AND
RADICAL THEOLOGIAN

"Jesus-followers who have stayed awake at night fearful of the second coming of Jesus need to read this book by Keith Giles! You'll be astounded with the idea of the 'Apocalyptic Hyperbole' and quickly come to see that there really is nothing to fear after all. In fact, the seeds of Jesus' divine presence live within you. The radical idea that the second coming has already occurred is a tremendous comfort to those who have been afflicted with fear and trembling about the rapture since their early days. I highly recommend this book to Christians who are ready to embrace a new truth about their faith journey so that you can live knowing the surprising reality of the second coming."

— REV. DR. KATY E. VALENTINE, AUTHOR OF *FOR YOU WERE BOUGHT WITH A PRICE: SEX, SLAVERY, AND SELF-CONTROL IN A PAULINE COMMUNITY* AND CO-HOST OF THE HERETIC HAPPY HOUR PODCAST

"All I can say is, wow! [*Jesus Unexpected*] packs quite a punch. The only issue I take is that the author didn't write it in the late 80s or early 90s, when I needed it most. It would have spared me from all the sleepless nights I had as a kid, worried that my parents would be raptured while I was 'left behind'. But I can forgive Giles for that because I know there are countless others still trapped in Dispensationalism, and it's better to find freedom late than to never find it at all."

— MATTHEW J. DISTEFANO, AUTHOR OF *HERETIC!* AND CO-HOST OF THE HERETIC HAPPY HOUR PODCAST

"In *Jesus Unexpected*, Keith unpacks the ideas of rapture theology, kingdom eventualities, and our place in all of it. Questions surrounding the biblical theories have been around for millennium and Keith jumps right in to share his take on the subject matter. As this topic was a source of existential crisis for me as a child, it is with great relief that I read of differing ideas as to the reality of this supposed event. I wanted to find those areas in which Keith had not done enough homework to disavow me of my preconceived ideas, but I was unable to identify an area in which he failed. As such, I found myself deeply interested and impressed with Keith's obvious attention to detail and his usual care in stating his standpoint."

— MICHELLE COLLINS, AUTHOR OF *INTO THE GRAY* AND HOST OF THE BOOK-ISH PODCAST

"Luther saw grave things wrong with the Church of his day. He posted his *96 Theses* calling out these atrocities and was branded a heretic and forced to live in exile. Had Keith Giles lived 500 years ago, he would also have been ostracized as a heretic and forced to live in exile. Let us be grateful that Keith is here now and that is not the case. Keith is a courageous modern-day Luther. He systematically takes us through the fallacies of the Church in his writings. In *Jesus Unexpected*, Keith does what he does best, exposing the modern-day myths about the End Times. He gives us this information in simple language, so that anyone of any age could read it and learn from it. When I read Keith's books, I feel like I am seated in a living room, relaxed, sipping coffee, and having an intelligent conversation with a friend. This friend is not out to prove everyone is wrong and he is right. He only desires for the reader to reconsider what they have been taught and seek truth and greater knowledge. I have needed this book for many years and I devoured every page of it!"

— TODD R. VICK, AUTHOR OF *THE RENEWING OF YOUR MIND* AND HOST OF THE RECONSTRUCTION REBEL PODCAST

"The subtitle of Keith Giles' new book says it all, *Jesus Unexpected: Ending the End Times to Become the Second Coming*. As is usual in his *Jesus Un* series, Keith keeps his author's eye on the ball—which in this case is a very present, pulsating, and palpable Jesus; a Christ who has already returned here in fullness to indwell all humanity. If true, and I think it largely is, this puts all futurist eschatology out of business. Keith's vibrant message to us is to look both 'within' ourselves and 'between' ourselves to find the unexpected Jesus—a Jesus whose eschatological timetable is always today, here, and now."

— RICHARD MURRAY, AUTHOR OF *GOD VERSUS EVIL: SCULPTING AN EPIC THEOLOGY OF GOD'S HEROIC GOODNESS*

"Those of us who were theologically formed in the era of the *Left Behind* series have been far more impacted than we realize by various end times conspiracy theories that many have come to view as Biblical truth. In *Jesus Unexpected*, Keith Giles masterfully dismantles these apocalyptic myths one by one. After laying waste to limiting false doctrines of the last days, Giles makes a compelling case for a far more hopeful view of the current state of the church and, in fact, the whole world.

Could it be that the climax of history is to be found not in our future but in the past? Could we be living in an era when all prophecies and hopes have already been fulfilled? How should we live in the days after 'the last days'?

[*Jesus Unexpected* is] Giles' most scholarly (yet completely approachable) work to date. His appendix on the dating of the book of Revelation is worth the price of the book all by itself."

— JASON ELAM, HOST OF THE MESSY SPIRITUALITY PODCAST

OTHER BOOKS BY THE AUTHOR

- *Jesus Undefeated: Condemning the False Doctrine of Eternal Torment*

- *Jesus Unveiled: Forsaking Church as We Know It for Ekklesia as God Intended*

- *Jesus Unbound: Liberating the Word of God from the Bible*

- *Jesus Untangled: Crucifying Our Politics to Pledge Allegiance to the Lamb*

- *The Power of Weakness: How God Loves to Do Extraordinary Things Through Ordinary People*

- *The Gospel: For Here or to Go?*

- *The Top 10 Things Every Christian Should Know (But Probably Doesn't)*

- *Nobody Follows Jesus (So Why Should You?)*

- *[Subversive Interviews] Volume 1*

- *War Is Not Christian*

- *How To Start A Ministry To The Poor In Your Own Community*

Available online at: www.KeithGiles.com

Copyright © 2020 by Keith Giles.

First Edition

Cover design and layout by Rafael Polendo (polendo.net)

ISBN 978-1-938480-65-2

This volume is printed on acid free paper and meets ANSI Z39.48 standards.

Printed in the United States of America

 QUOIR

Published by Quoir
Oak Glen, California

www.quoir.com

JESUS
UNEXPECTED
ENDING THE END TIMES TO BECOME THE SECOND COMING

KEITH GILES

SPECIAL THANKS

Rafael Polendo, Bram Watkins, Brad Jersak, Wm. Paul Young, Greg Boyd, Richard Murray, Dr. Katy Valentine, Matthew Distefano, Michelle Collins, Todd Vick, David Bentley Hart, Steve Gregg, Ken Gentry, and Greg Bahnsen.

DEDICATION

To my sons, Dylan and David. I pray you never doubt that you are dearly loved more than you could possibly imagine.

TABLE OF CONTENTS

FOREWORD

"And though St. John the Evangelist saw many strange monsters in his vision, he saw no creature so wild as one of his own commentators."

— G. K. CHESTERTON

To be perfectly honest, I have never been interested in studying "the end times" or "the second coming of Christ," what scholars call "eschatology." I have read my fair share of the views offered, of course, and listened to hours and hours of discussions, sometimes very heated discussions, about "what the Bible is saying." But, with few exceptions, the views espoused all made the same catastrophic mistake. They assumed the real absence of Jesus *now*. They assumed that the human race is separated from Jesus Christ. They assumed that his kingdom was out there, over there, or up there and soon to come, maybe. But what if we assumed—with the apostles—that Jesus is really here now, with us, in us and us in him? What would happen to our eschatology if we believed that the Son who is one with his Father, full of the Holy Spirit, the Creator and sustainer of all things, the victorious Lamb, the great High Priest who was dead but now everlastingly alive, is fully and personally present now and forever? Apart from the giant flush we would hear across the eschatological cosmos all the questions would dramatically change. Perhaps new questions would emerge, with new insights flashing like lightning across our minds, which quickened us with unearthly assurance. And perhaps we would begin to see God, ourselves, our enemies with Jesus' eyes, and feel with his heart.

Is Jesus worried right now that the dragon and the beasts or the great whore of Babylon may after all win the day? Does he bite his fingernails in anxiety as to how things will turn out on planet earth? The apostles declare to the world that Jesus Christ sits face to face with the Father, above all rule and authority in this age and in all ages to come. John portrays Jesus as a little lamb, alive as if slain in the middle of the throne of all thrones. Do you think Jesus is overwhelmed with angst right now? Is his soul baptized in fear? Looking into the eyes of His Father, baptized with the unlimited joy of the Holy Spirit, Jesus is aflame with hope. What if this Jesus is with us, in us, and we with and in him? What if Immanuel is not a theory, but an abiding reality? What if we are in him now as he is seated above all rule and authority in the sea of shalom? That gives a new context to Jesus' command, "abide in Me," does it not? And does it not give a new framework to eschatology, which may not be new at all?

> THE DISASTER OF BAD ESCHATOLOGY IS NOT ONLY WHAT IT TEACHES, BUT WHAT IT KEEPS US FROM SEEING, FROM SEEING THAT WHICH IS TOO BEAUTIFUL FOR WORDS, THE LAMB UPON HIS THRONE NOW, AND US IN HIM NOW.

The disaster of bad eschatology is not only what it teaches, but what it keeps us from seeing, from seeing that which is too beautiful for words, the Lamb upon his throne now, and us in him now. Without such a breathtaking vision we end up not full of hope, but forced to pretend, to entertain ourselves with dazzling worship, or doomed to strike a pose where we appear to be relevant. But isn't this simply playing church? Is this not creating a make believe kingdom out of our own resources? Does such a loss of light do anything to deliver us from fear, or the presumptuous pride that we indeed are "in" and most others are "out." Without the vision of the Lamb in the midst of the throne of all thrones—and us in him—are we not consigning ourselves to become bored with our own rhetoric, or, as Lewis said, to becoming "half-hearted creatures, fooling about with drink and sex and ambition when infinite joy is offered us, like an ignorant child who wants to go on making mud pies in a slum because he cannot imagine what is meant by the offer of a holiday at the sea. We are far too easily pleased" (*The Weight of Glory*, p. 2).

In *Jesus Unexpected: Ending the End Times to Become the Second Coming,* Keith Giles takes a look at the questions of eschatology from the perspective that Jesus is fully and really present now.

> "Jesus has returned. He is alive within you. Living and breathing inside your skin. You are His hands. You are His feet. You are what all creation has been rooting for. Not later. Now. Not one day. Today. What is the hope of glory? It is Christ in you!" (p.189).

If this is true, if the gospel of Paul—Christ in you—is true, then how did we get so far off base? How did we so misinterpret John as to transform the book of the Revelation of Jesus Christ into such a grotesque monster that most Christians simply avoid in fear?

I for one would love to read answers to these questions. And what about Jesus' famous Olivet Discourse? And the 70 weeks of Daniel's prophecy, the Abomination of Desolation, the mark of the beast, the anti-Christ, the day of the Lord, and the so-called "second coming of Jesus?" Thankfully, Giles takes on these questions and topics with uncomplicated simplicity. If we adjust our assumptions, assumptions about Jesus' presence, things line up beautifully. If not, we plunge ourselves into endless squabble not only with others but with our own hearts, and we know not the divine peace that comes from seeing ourselves in the little lamb in the center of the throne. Giles takes the road less traveled, at least in these "modern" times, and he helps us see Jesus with us and in us, and us with and in him. This is eschatology at its best.

– C. Baxter Kruger, Ph.D.

Author of the international bestsellers *The Shack Revisited,* and *Patmos.*

INTRODUCTION

"The information in the book you're about to read is more up-to-date than tomorrow's newspaper. I can say this with confidence because the facts and predictions in the next few pages are all taken from the greatest sourcebook of current events in the world."

– HAL LINDSEY[1], *THERE'S A NEW WORLD COMING* (1973)

Daniel sat up in his bed. It was a little after 3 AM on a Tuesday. There was rain pattering against his window. The wind outside was rustling the tree leaves in the front yard. He could hear the clock ticking in the hallway outside his bedroom door. The silence between those spaces was terrifying.

What frightened him most is what he *couldn't* hear. Were his parents still in the house? What if they had been taken in the night? What if he had been left behind? The fear of being alone in this world, abandoned by God, and his parents, slowly began to swell within his little chest and made his blood run cold.

He knew he wasn't always a good Christian boy. Sometimes he told dirty jokes to his friends at school to make them laugh. Other times he had used bad words to impress his classmates. He once stole a *Playboy* magazine from underneath his uncle's bed when they were visiting one Thanksgiving weekend and nearly got caught trying to hide it from his mother. *What if Jesus came back last night? What if his parents were raptured and his sins weren't covered in the blood of Christ? How would he survive the Tribulation? What horrors would he have to face without the comfort and protection of his parents?*

Daniel had seen those movies about the End Times at an all-night youth lock-in a few years ago. He remembered the scenes where 100-pound hailstones fell out of the sky and crushed people to death. He remembered these fearsome creatures that crawled out of the Abyss to torment people day and night. The soldiers who came to round up the ones who wouldn't bow down to the Anti-Christ would probably find him eventually, he thought.

But, maybe everything was ok? Maybe he was just being paranoid? Daniel took a deep breath and found enough courage to slip out of bed, one foot at a time. He slowly inched his way out of his bedroom and into the hallway where he stopped and stood very still. The only sounds were of the clock, the rain on the window, and the pounding of his own heart inside his chest.

After a moment, he crept down the hallway towards his parent's bedroom. His bare feet were silent on the carpeted floor. With every step he paused to listen for a sign but heard nothing.

Finally, Daniel was right up to his parent's bedroom door. He leaned forward and placed his ear against it. At first, he heard nothing, but then, at last, he heard his father snoring softly. One of them—he couldn't tell if it was his mom or his dad—shifted their weight and the bed gently creaked. That sound was like music to his ears. His heart flooded with relief. The tension and fear in his body began to subside. He took another breath to savor the comfort of knowing he wasn't alone in the house, and slowly turned to walk back to the comfort of his bed.

Scenes like this one played out in Daniel's house several times a month. Constantly unsure of his standing with God, he would often awaken in the middle of the night, listen for signs of his parents sleeping, become flooded with fearful images of an End Times nightmare, and have to venture out of bed to reassure himself that the Rapture hadn't taken his parents away in the night.

But Daniel isn't the only young person who has lived with this constant fear of being left behind. Thousands of other children have also struggled with these fears. I was one of them. Maybe you were too?

The fact is these same fears have paralyzed both young and old alike for over a hundred years now. Especially in America where the Dispensational doctrine of the End Times Rapture has taken a strong hold over the hearts and minds of Evangelical Christians.

THE FACT IS THESE SAME FEARS HAVE PARALYZED BOTH YOUNG AND OLD ALIKE FOR OVER A HUNDRED YEARS NOW. ESPECIALLY IN AMERICA WHERE THE DISPENSATIONAL DOCTRINE OF THE END TIMES RAPTURE HAS TAKEN A STRONG HOLD OVER THE HEARTS AND MINDS OF EVANGELICAL CHRISTIANS.

But it hasn't always been this way. Many Christians have no idea that this last days scenario of a coming Anti-Christ who forces everyone to take the Mark of the Beast and rebuilds the Temple in Jerusalem so he can declare himself God and persecutes Christians until Jesus returns to rescue them in a battle so fierce that the blood rises to the bridles of the war horses in the valley of Armageddon is something no Christian ever believed until roughly 1830.

That's why I'm writing this book: to explain where we got these ideas from, why they're not anything we need to lose sleep over, and how this teaching actually distracts us from following God's plan for His Church in these last days.

To accomplish this, I'll be breaking things down into sections. First, we will look at where these ideas about the End

Times originate from and how they became synonymous with American Christianity over the last 180 years. Next, we will examine each of the major prophecies found in both the Old and the New Testament scriptures to determine what they're actually pointing to, whether they have been fulfilled or not, and if so, how, and if not, what remains unfulfilled today. Finally, once we've cleared away all the confusion and hype, we'll take a look at what the Bible really *does* tell us about the Second Coming of Christ, the New Jerusalem, the End Times temple, and the future of mankind according to the prophecy of Jesus and the revelation of the New Testament.

This will not be an easy topic for us to explore. There are numerous concepts we'll need to examine from various angles. Some of our preconceptions about what the Scriptures have to say about the Second Coming of Christ and the End Times will need to be scrutinized and re-considered critically. Our fears about the Apocalypse may be challenged. Our hopes for a future Millennial Reign may be shattered. Our assumptions about what the Bible says will happen at the end of time may be radically shifted by the time we're through. I hope you're up for this.

CHAPTER 1

THE ORIGIN OF THE END TIMES HYPE

"I imagine the later Gentile [Church] Fathers were at a disadvantage in understanding Hebrew idioms. This probably adversely affected their grasp of some prophecies, just as the same deficiency has afflicted modern interpreters. However, modern scholarship has shed a lot of light on these matters, and we are in a pretty good position to exegete the passages."

— STEVE GREGG[1]

We all sat around on the floor in my friend's living room. Everyone had a Bible open in their lap. Our teacher, only a few years older than the rest of us, sat cross-legged on the carpet. He was wearing a black Harley-Davidson t-shirt and brown cut-off shorts. His feet were bare. A scruff of beard stubble graced his chin. In one hand he held a copy of a brand-new book about the End Times. I could read the title in giant red bold print across the front, *88 Reasons Why the Rapture Will Be In 1988* by Edgar C. Whisenant.

Over the next hour and a half, our teacher breathlessly expounded on each of those 88 reasons and hammered each of them home with a pointed finger that pierced the air between us. Everyone in the room was riveted by what we were hearing.

How could we not be enthralled? Jesus was returning in just a few more months! The very idea was electrifying and sobering all at once. Many of us were trying to wrap our brains around the fact that we would never get married, have children, grow old, or live our lives the way we had hoped.

To be honest, most of us left that meeting feeling fearful and sad rather than encouraged or hopeful. Our lives were over before they had really begun. At least, they were if this prophecy was true.

But, of course, it wasn't true. 1988 came and went and Jesus did not part the sky and come riding down from heaven on a white stallion with a sword in his mouth as we had been told. This was yet another failed prophecy in a very, very long line of failed prophecies about the Second Coming of Christ that had made a mockery of the scriptures and fools of everyone who had taken them seriously.

In 1989 the very same author we had studied published a follow-up book with the un-ironic title: *89 Reasons Why the Rapture Will Be In 1989*. As you might suspect, this new edition didn't sell nearly as well, even though it produced exactly the same results: total and complete failure to understand what the Bible had to say about the End Times, the Second Coming of Christ and the End of the World.

IN FACT, THIS BRAND OF TEACHING HAS ONE THING IN COMMON, REGARDLESS OF WHO THE AUTHOR OR TEACHER HAPPENS TO BE: THEY ALL FAIL TO GET IT RIGHT. ALL OF THEM. EVERY SINGLE TIME.

In fact, this brand of teaching has one thing in common, regardless of who the author or teacher happens to be: They all fail to get it right. All of them. Every single time. And yet, in spite of this unbroken series of failures, there has been no end to the books, conferences or teaching on this topic over the last hundred years or so. As we begin to examine *Failed End Times Biblical Prophecies* throughout history, we'll see a very disturbing pattern beginning to emerge:[2]

THE GREAT DISAPPOINTMENT: OCTOBER 22, 1844

In the 19th Century, William Miller began preaching that the Rapture was going to take place on October 22, 1844. An estimated 100,000 Americans gathered around the country on this date in anticipation of Christ's return and this failed prophecy became widely known as "The Great Disappointment." Miller died five years later having renounced his Biblical Prophecy studies, but people continued to meet together in spite of the obvious failure of his teachings and one of those religious groups became known as the Seventh Day Adventist denomination.

THE WATCHTOWER BIBLE AND TRACT SOCIETY: 1925

In 1918, Jehovah's Witnesses president, J.F. Rutherford predicted the return of Jesus and the end of the world would come in 1925, saying,

> "…We may confidently expect that 1925 will mark the return of Abraham, Isaac, Jacob and the faithful prophets of old, particularly those named by the Apostle in Hebrews 11, to the condition of human perfection."

This failed prophecy did little to hinder the growth or popularity of the movement which continued to set dates for the Second Coming of Christ and the end of the world for several years afterwards.

HAROLD CAMPING: 1994 AND 2011

As the President of Family Radio, Harold Camping said that he was "99.9% certain" that Jesus was returning in 1994. This prophecy was based on a very random and convoluted series of mathematical calculations using various numbers found in the

Bible. When this first prophecy about 1994 didn't come to pass, Camping repeated his error by predicting the return of Jesus on May 21, 2011. When this also failed to occur, Camping responded by saying,

> "We must listen to Jesus when he says that we must always be prepared for the end because it might happen at any moment— though it could also take place in the distant future."

DAVID MEADE: OCTOBER 15, 2017 AND APRIL 23, 2018

David Meade, a self-professed Christian Numerologist, made several predictions for the return of Christ and the end of the world using astronomy, Bible verses and creative exegesis. First, he predicted that the end would come on October 15, 2017 saying,

> When the birth of Jupiter from Virgo occurs, we also see the fulfillment of Genesis 3:15 and Revelation 12:4 when great and fearful signs in the heavens are given… This birthing occurs according to the latest astronomical data available on October 15, 2017. This is when the King Planet—Jupiter, crosses the womb region of Virgo."

When this prediction failed, Meade went on to claim that April 23 of 2018 was the date of the end, and then backpedaled from that a few days later saying that the end was still *"coming soon."*[3]

These are only a handful of failed End Times prophecies over the last hundred years. The sad truth is that there are so many examples of these false prophecies about the end times and the return of Christ that one could quite easily write an entire book about this topic alone.

These sorts of predictions pop up with such regularity that we've become indifferent to them. We roll our eyes, marvel that so many people seem to fall for it and shake our heads in disgust when those dates come and go. But perhaps we have had seasons in our life when we *did* believe it. We listened to those preachers and we absorbed their theories with absolute confidence. Maybe we became so obsessed with these predictions that we even did something radical like quit our jobs, sell our houses, or move to the mountains to await the End of the World.

Even if we didn't do such drastic things, there are hundreds of Christians who have taken such life-altering steps in anticipation of the Second Coming. When the dates came and went, they were left feeling disillusioned and ripped off. Many lost their faith in God entirely and walked away from anything having to do with Christ or Christianity.

The destructive nature of these endless failed prophecies is difficult to measure, but real nonetheless. Yet, none of this seems to prevent the next person from writing their book about the signs of the Second Coming. Nor does it seem to negatively impact the popularity of such practices.

APPARENTLY, ONE CAN BE QUITE SUCCESSFUL WRITING BOOKS AND SETTING DATES THAT CONTINUALLY FAIL TO PRODUCE ANY ACCURATE RESULTS WHEN IT COMES TO PREDICTING THE FUTURE OR CONNECTING BIBLICAL PROPHECIES TO CURRENT EVENTS.

Apparently, one can be quite successful writing books and setting dates that continually fail to produce any accurate results when it comes to predicting the future or connecting Biblical prophecies to current events. Just ask people like John Hagee, Hal Lindsey, Tim LaHaye, and dozens more who continually publish books about Biblical Prophecy that eventually end up in the sale bins after the dates they have predicted fail to materialize; books that are merely replaced by a new title a few years later, promising even greater revelation about the return of Christ than ever before.

Why is this? Why don't people wise up and stop handing over their money to these failed prophets of the End Times? Maybe it's because our appetite for knowing the future is greater than our capacity to think critically or use common sense. At any rate, many Christians seem to be addicted to knowing exactly how close we are to the second coming of Jesus and are totally convinced that we are living in the last days.

But how did we become so easily convinced? Has it always been this way? No, it hasn't. In fact, this end times hype and futurist vision of Biblical prophecy is relatively new.

Most Christians are unaware that for the majority of Church history, most Christians did not believe that there were specific events in the Middle East that needed to take place before Christ would physically return to rapture his followers and judge the world. This teaching only became popularized in 1830—the same year that Joseph Smith introduced Mormonism—and was promoted by a man named John Nelson Darby in England as Dispensational Theology.

So, what is Dispensational Theology? Where did Darby's ideas come from? What specific concepts were introduced into Christianity as the result of his new ideas? And how did those ideas so quickly become incorporated into American Christianity and eventually come to be accepted as normal Christian Theology? Let's examine those questions and look a bit closer at Dispensationalism and how it has come to shape our modern ideas about the End Times, the return of Christ and the End of the World.

CHAPTER 2

DARBY AND THE DISPENSATIONAL FUTURISTS

"The decade of the 80's may be the last generation of our era."
— HAL LINDSEY[1]

As we have already mentioned, Dispensationalism was formulated by a man named John Nelson Darby in 1829.

John Nelson Darby was born in Westminster, London, March 3, 1801. He was the youngest of six sons and was educated at Westminster School and Trinity College, Dublin. While he embraced Christianity during his studies, there is no evidence that he formally studied theology, although he was tutored by the future Bishop of Meath and evangelical pastor named Joseph Singer while he was at Trinity College.

In 1826, he was ordained in the Church of Ireland as a priest, although he resigned in protest when converts were required to pledge an oath to King George IV. Soon afterwards, in October 1827, Darby fell from his horse and was seriously injured. According to Darby, it was during this time that he began to believe that the kingdom described in the Book of Isaiah and elsewhere in the Old Testament was entirely different from the

Christian church. This teaching about the separation between Israel and the Church is one of the earmarks of what would eventually become Dispensationalism. We'll explore this in detail later.

Over the next five years, Darby developed the principles of his Dispensational theology and began meeting with others who shared his particular views. By 1832, this group had grown and began to identify itself as a distinct Christian assembly, founding other groups across Ireland and England. This eventually became known as the Plymouth Brethren.

Darby left the Church of Ireland in 1831 and began to participate in an annual Bible Conference organized by his friend, Lady Powerscourt, a wealthy widow. At these conferences Darby began to publicly describe his unique eschatological views which included teachings about the pretribulation rapture. Because of this, Darby has been credited with originating the pretribulation rapture theory which teaches that Christ will suddenly appear and remove the Church from the earth into heaven immediately before the end times judgments of sinners known as the Tribulation. This teaching, which underpins Christian Zionism, assumes that God's prophetic plan involves the ethnic Jewish nation of Israel and presupposes that there are unfulfilled prophecies concerning the Jewish people that must take place in the future, prior to the second coming of Jesus.

According to Dispensational Theology, "...while the ways of God may change, His purposes to bless Israel will never be forgotten, just as He has shown unmerited favour to the Church, He will do so to a remnant of Israel to fulfill all the promises made to the genetic seed of Abraham." [2]

But whereas Darby may have formulated these views and packaged them as "Dispensationalism," he wasn't exactly the originator. Instead, it turns out that much of it was inspired by the fever dream of a dying woman named Margaret McDonald in Scotland.[3]

A decade prior to Darby's formal invention of Dispensationalism, there was a Presbyterian minister from London in 1820 named Edward Irving who essentially gave rise to modern-day Pentecostalism. Two years prior to being kicked out of the Presbyterian denomination, Irving was preaching and promoting the practice of spiritual gifts at a revival in Scotland. During one of those services, a woman named Margaret McDonald, who was deathly ill, came under the power of the Holy Spirit and gave them a "mingled prophecy and vision" about how the End Times were soon going to unfold.[4]

LATER, AS DARBY BEGAN PREACHING THIS NEWLY-FORMED DOOMSDAY THEOLOGY, THERE WAS ONE NOTABLE YOUNG PERSON IN HIS CONGREGATION WHO WAS GREATLY IMPACTED BY THIS TEACHING. HIS NAME WAS ALEISTER CROWLEY.

According to Margaret's prophetic word, the return of Jesus would be in two stages—not one. The first would be a secret rapture for true believers, and then after a period of great tribulation, Jesus would return a second time for all to see.

There is evidence that Darby heard of this and, although not in favor of the spiritual gifts aspect of this movement, he actually visited Margaret McDonald's home to hear firsthand about this brand new prophecy of the end of the world.[5]

After listening to her story, Darby was able to formulate a version of this revelation that made all of Margaret's new ideas seemingly fit together scripturally.

THE CROWLEY-DARBY CONNECTION

Later, as Darby began preaching this newly-formed doomsday theology, there was one notable young person in his congregation who was greatly impacted by this teaching. His name was Aleister Crowley.

In case you're not aware, Crowley is a very famous occultist and is considered by many to be "one of the *wickedest men in the world.*"

According to a pro-Crowley website, Darby's theology had a negative effect on the young boy. Here's a bit of detail taken from a pro-Crowley website that sheds some light on this Darby-Crowley connection:

> "When other children attended the Presbyterian church to listen and fantasize about angels with halos, or Moses parting the Red Sea destroying the armies of Egypt, Crowley sat there transfixed listening to Darby... tell the faithful attendees of the rewards of heaven and the magical rapture. Of the evil and terrible day when those that did not put their trust in Jesus were left behind. Left behind to suffer in the hands of the Antichrist and the Beast; beheading or torture their only way to salvation.
>
> As a boy, Crowley was given a dose of the message that millions of evangelical Christians would listen to in the future. During Crowley's childhood, The Rapture was not widespread. The End-Time scenario, Rapture, Antichrist and his horrible tribulation, and the gnashing of teeth was not your run of the mill evangelical doctrine but something exclusive to a handful of churches, one which little Aleister Crowley happened to attend.
>
> Crowley rebelled against this absurd doomsday scenario. He was one of the first to do so. He rebelled in an age where this doomsday scenario was not a widespread phenomenon like it is today. I can only imagine what being part of a doomsday cult was like during his boyhood.
>
> The thing is... we know how Crowley turned out after listening to Darby's interpretation of the fate of mankind in his early years. Now that the great majority of Protestants believe in the Rapture myth and every doomsday death wish that this entitles them to, I wonder... how many Crowley's is the modern

Protestant movement—basically millions of clones of Darby's church—creating? Time will tell. I think Crowley was just the first fruit."[6]

So, thanks to John Nelson Darby, we not only inherited an end times theology that regularly spawns date-setting "end of the world" predictions—which always fail, of course—and an entire cottage industry for those who claim to know the identity of the anti-Christ, or how some future events will bring us tantalizingly closer to the return of Christ, we also have Darby to thank for the twisted ideas of someone like Aleister Crowley.

Who knows how many others like him—who heard a version of the Gospel that was built on fear and conjecture, and that chases signs of the end of the world—are turned away from the true message of Christ?

DISPENSATIONALISM IN AMERICA

At any rate, after Darby's teaching began to find a home in Ireland and England, he travelled extensively to establish assemblies across Europe between 1830 and 1840. Eventually, Darby made his way to America between 1862 and 1877 and worked primarily in New England and the Great Lakes area of the United States, establishing assemblies and followers along the way.

DARBY'S ESCHATOLOGY AND VIEWS ABOUT ISRAEL AND THE END TIMES WERE WIDELY POPULARIZED IN AMERICA BY CYRUS SCOFIELD'S *SCOFIELD REFERENCE BIBLE* PUBLISHED BY OXFORD UNIVERSITY PRESS IN 1909, A FEW YEARS BEFORE WORLD WAR I.

Darby's eschatology and views about Israel and the End Times were widely popularized in America by Cyrus Scofield's *Scofield Reference Bible* published by Oxford University Press in 1909, a few years before World War I.

In fact, it was the inclusion of Darby's ideas in this Bible which seems to have single-handedly seared the American Christian conscience with the doctrine of Dispensationalism.

As some historians have put it, "Historically speaking, the *Scofield Reference Bible* was to dispensationalism what Luther's *Ninety-five Theses* was to Lutheranism, or what Calvin's *Institutes* was to Calvinism." [7]

EARLY CRITICS

While many eventually embraced Darby's ideas in America, there were several notable Christian teachers who did not. Most famously, noted pastor and author Charles H. Spurgeon was one of Darby's most passionate detractors. Spurgeon's greatest concern was for how Darby's new theology "rejected the vicarious purpose of Christ's obedience as well as imputed righteousness." [8] Spurgeon viewed these doctrines as being of such importance and so central to the Gospel that it led him to publish a much longer statement about the entirety of Darby's theology in which he accused him of "laboring to seduce the members of our churches to the subversion of the truth and the overthrow of the needful order and discipline of our Zion," and referred to the teaching as "among the darkest signs of the times." [9]

And James Grant, whose detailed rebuttal of Darby's theology was published by Spurgeon's own *Sword and Trowel* periodical in 1860 said in his summary of Dispensationalism:

> "With the deadly heresies entertained and taught by the Plymouth Brethren [Darbyites], in relation to some of the most momentous of all the doctrines of the Gospel, and to which I have adverted at some length, I feel assured that my readers will not be surprised at any other views, however unscriptural and pernicious they may be, which the Darbyites have embraced and zealously seek to propagate."

However, in spite of such notable opponents to Darby's Dispensationalism at the time, the concepts introduced by Darby were eventually embraced on a much wider scale, especially due to the popularity of the *Scofield Reference Bible* and the notes containing Darby's theology contained in the margins.

As these concepts continued to permeate through the American Christian Church, there were several Christian Seminaries and Bible Colleges that openly embraced and promoted Darby's views. This led to several hundred thousand pastors (and counting) being indoctrinated into Dispensational teachings concerning the End Times and Pretribulation Rapture Theory.

Because of this, Dispensationalism's grip on the American Christian Church has become so pervasive that many average Christians totally embrace the theology without ever knowing who Darby was or that much of their theology originated in the 1830's.

SPECIFIC CONCEPTS

While Darby's entire theology is indeed complicated and convoluted at times, what we are most specifically concerned with in this book involves two main concepts that drive our modern-day preoccupation with the Second Coming of Christ. So, we're not going to spend any time explaining any of the other nuances of Dispensationalism which looks at Scripture through various lenses and divides events into dispensations, or any of the other theological particulars of this view. Our focus here will be narrowly confined to teachings that have influenced modern Christian ideas about the End Times.

The two teachings of Dispensationalism we want to take time to explore here are: *The Identity of Israel* (according to the New

Testament), and the *End Times Narrative* (according to a specific reading of certain prophetic passages in both the Old and the New Testament scriptures).

These are the primary concepts introduced and popularized by Darby in 1830 that have come to shape Christian Eschatology in the American Church today. So, let's take a look at each one in turn and try to understand why they're significant, and how exactly they have shaped the way we understand scriptures in our Bibles that speak about the End Times.

CHAPTER 3

ISRAEL AND THE CHURCH

"Assemblies that worship God in spirit and in truth, are the Israel of God"

— MATTHEW HENRY

WHO IS ISRAEL?

Before we get too deep into this topic, I do need to say a few things up front. First of all, there are numerous examples throughout church history of Christians persecuting Jewish people in horrific ways. Many of those who did so justified such violence by pointing to New Testament passages that say the Jews were the ones who killed Jesus, or by referencing scriptures that speak of God's judgement being poured out on the Jewish people for rejecting the Gospel. This is unacceptable. No one who follows Jesus should ever oppress or violently attack anyone at any time, for any reason.

Second of all, we must understand that as we look at the passages that draw a distinction between Jews and Christians, or between Israel and the Church, we are not falling into agreement or alignment with any of those who seek to exercise their hatred against the Jewish people.

Simply put, Christians love Jewish people and I love the Jewish people. I do not approve of anyone who wants to attack, oppress or disparage the Jewish faith, or Jewish people, in any way, shape or form. So, please do not take what we are about to explore as an attack on Jewish people. In fact, please try to keep in mind that Jesus was Jewish, and that the Apostle Paul was Jewish, and so were the Twelve Disciples, and the majority of the original Christians all throughout the earliest days of Christianity. Therefore, whenever we read something that Jesus or Paul or one of the other Apostles says about Israel or about the Jewish people, we are listening to an in-house conversation where members of one family talk about others within their own ethnic and religious family. They are not attempting to create walls of division between people as much as they are attempting to make sense of God's prophetic fulfillment of promises made to the nation of Israel long ago. This is where we should do our best to try to see things purely from a prophetic perspective and not from a personal one.

> SO, PLEASE DO NOT TAKE WHAT WE ARE ABOUT TO EXPLORE AS AN ATTACK ON JEWISH PEOPLE. IN FACT, PLEASE TRY TO KEEP IN MIND THAT JESUS WAS JEWISH, AND THAT THE APOSTLE PAUL WAS JEWISH, AND SO WERE THE TWELVE DISCIPLES, AND THE MAJORITY OF THE ORIGINAL CHRISTIANS ALL THROUGHOUT THE EARLIEST DAYS OF CHRISTIANITY.

Having said this, the identity of Israel is an especially significant question we need to explore if we hope to understand prophetic scriptures in both the Old and the New Testament. Paul thought so, too. This is why he spent a lot of time in the Epistles to the Galatians and to the Romans explaining this concept in great detail.

Here's why it matters who Israel is: Because God made some specific promises to Israel, and until we know to whom those promises were made, we can't know whether or not those promises were fulfilled. For example, if Israel refers to ethnic Jews, then we'll need to determine whether the promises were fulfilled for them. But, if Israel is defined using some other criteria, we need to know what that might be and then we can see if those promises were fulfilled for those who meet those conditions.

For John Nelson Darby, Israel is defined very simply as anyone who was born into an ethnically Jewish family. In other words, any Jewish person is automatically included in the group known as Israel. The two are synonymous. So, taking that as the starting point, any promise made to Israel in the Old Testament is only truly fulfilled if we can see that it was something experienced by the Jewish people at some point in history. If not, then according to Darby and to those who embrace Dispensational Theology, the promise is not yet fulfilled.

However, if Israel is defined for us in another way, then perhaps we might want to consider how this is applied when it comes to the promises and prophecies about Israel in the Old Testament.

Fair enough? Ok, here's where we need to pay attention to how the Apostle Paul defines "Israel" in his epistles, and then look at how he applies those promises and prophecies to those who fit his specific definition.

To start things off, Paul actually begins by defining who Israel is *not*. As we read in Romans 2:28

> "For he is not a Jew [Israel] who is one outwardly, nor is circumcision that of the flesh."

Here we see that being considered a Jew requires more than outward appearance, or even privately in terms of being circumcised. As notable scholar A.W. Pink says:

"What could be plainer than that? In the light of such a Scripture, is it not passing strange that there are today those boasting loudly of their orthodoxy and bitterly condemning all who differ—who insist that the name 'Jew' belongs only to the natural descendants of Jacob...?"[1]

Again, what is in view here is merely prophetic fulfillment. Obviously, anyone who is naturally born into the Jewish ethnicity is a Jew. That's not what Paul means to suggest here. Keeping in mind that Paul was a Jew himself, we need to take a step back and understand that the goal here is to understand *to whom* those Old Testament promises applied to? Paul wants us to understand that they were made not merely to those who were outwardly Jewish, but that God had something much more specific in mind.

SO, THE IDENTITY OF "ISRAEL" IS NOT DEFINED BY ONE'S ETHNICITY OR RACE. THIS SEEMS TO BE AN IMPORTANT POINT THAT THE APOSTLE PAUL WANTS US TO UNDERSTAND BEFORE MOVING ON TO EXPLAIN WHO ISRAEL ACTUALLY REFERS TO IN TERMS OF THESE PROPHETIC PROMISES.

To further clarify his point, Paul went on to explain in Romans 9:6-8 who was, and was not, Israel:

"For they are not all Israel who are descended from Israel; nor are they all children because they are Abraham's descendants... That is, it is not the children of the flesh who are children of God, but the children of the promise are regarded as descendants."

As Dr. Charles Hodge says in his commentary on this passage:

"...the promise was not addressed to the mere natural descendants of Abraham. For they are not all Israel which are of Israel, i.e. all the natural descendants of the patriarch are not the true people of God... All descendants from the patriarch Jacob called Israel, are not the true people of God; [in the same way] all who are in the visible church [who are members of a local congregation] do not belong to the true invisible church."[2]

So, the identity of "Israel" is not defined by one's ethnicity or race. This seems to be an important point that the Apostle Paul wants us to understand before moving on to explain who Israel actually refers to in terms of these prophetic promises.

One Biblical scholar, Gregory Bahnsen, wrote about this distinction made by Paul in Romans and admitted it was challenging for some to grasp, but also pointed out that Jesus made a similar distinction:

"This may be the hardest section for some to swallow. [But] Jesus stated something vitally important to the Jews of his day in their dialogue with Him found in the eighth chapter of John, verses 33-44.

"Starting at verse 33, the Jews declared they were the seed of Abraham. Jesus responded by saying that He knew they were the (natural) seed of Abraham and then stated, 'but ye seek to kill me, because my word has no place in you'. He then adds why His word has no place with them, 'I speak that which I have seen with my Father: and you do that which ye have seen with your father'. Then, again, the Jews declared, 'Abraham is our father'. Jesus rebuked their false view of what it means to be a child of Abraham by stating, 'If ye were Abraham's children, ye would do the works of Abraham', and proceeds to state that Abraham would not seek to kill Him. In fact, he stated that Abraham rejoiced to see His [Christ's] day (John 8:56). Jesus explained "*if*" you were the children of Abraham, you would rejoice to see my day, henceforth, since you do not rejoice to see my day, you are *not* the Children of Abraham."[3]

So, both Paul and Jesus make a distinction between those who are merely born into the lineage of Abraham, and those who are spiritually Abraham's children based on what was in their heart.

Therefore, one could be born into a Jewish family and still fail to meet the criteria for "A Child of Abraham" in God's eyes. And one could be born into a Gentile family and still qualify as "A Child of Abraham," based on one's heart. What makes the difference is the heart and the spirit of that person. In other words, "man looks at the outward appearance, but God looks at the heart."[4]

This means it's not the physical DNA of a person that matters, but the spiritual identity of a person who has been transformed by the love of Christ.

WHO IS TRUE ISRAEL?

Paul defines Israel for us in Romans 2:29:

> "But he is a Jew, which is one inwardly; and circumcision is that of the heart, in the spirit, and not in the letter; whose praise is not of men, but God."

Jewish males defined themselves, in large part, by the physical act of circumcision which was a sign for them. Here, Paul makes the distinction between physical circumcision, performed in the flesh, and a circumcision of the heart that is performed by the Holy Spirit on a spiritual level. Therefore, a Jew (meaning the person to whom those promises may apply) is defined inwardly, not outwardly; spiritually, not physically.

Other Biblical commentators and scholars affirm this distinction, including Matthew Henry who said: "Assemblies that worship God in spirit and in truth, are the Israel of God,"[5] and Matthew Poole who affirmed that "…he is a right and true Jew, an Israelite indeed…that worships God in Spirit, rejoices in Christ Jesus…Such are the [true] circumcision and Jew."[6]

The Apostle Paul further argued his point in the epistle to the Galatians, one of his earliest letters, and quite possibly the first one he wrote after his conversion to the Christian faith. In this letter he explicitly refers to the original promise made to

Abraham by God in Genesis 15:5-6 and applies it to anyone who is in Christ.

> "Just as Abraham 'believed God, and it was reckoned to him as righteousness,' so, you see, *those who believe are the descendants of Abraham.*" (Gal. 3:6-7) [emphasis mine]

> "*Now the promises were made to Abraham and to his seed*; it does not say, 'And to seeds,' as of many; but it says, 'And to your seed,' that is, to one person, *who is Christ.*" (Gal. 3:16) [emphasis mine]

> "*As many of you as were baptized into Christ have clothed yourselves with Christ.* There is no longer Jew or Greek, there is no longer slave or free, there is no longer male and female; for all of you are one in Christ Jesus. *And if you belong to Christ, then you are Abraham's seed, and heirs according to the promise.*" (Gal. 3:27-29) [emphasis mine]

Hopefully you can follow Paul's train of thought here. He begins by quoting from the original promise made to Abraham by God in Genesis 15:5-6, (mentioned in Gal. 3:6), and then says that those who believe or have faith in Christ "are the descendants of Abraham." This is a pretty radical statement. But, he's not finished yet.

In Galatians 3:16 he goes on to say that "the promises were made to Abraham and his seed", which up until now most assumed only meant those who were ethnically Jewish. But Paul corrects this by pointing out that the promise was not made to a plural *"seeds"* but to a singular *"seed"* and this is none other than Christ.

Finally, Paul wraps up his argument by saying that anyone "baptized into Christ" has "clothed [themselves] with Christ", and then drops the final bomb by asserting that "…if you belong to Christ, then you are Abraham's seed, and heirs according to the promise." This is a mic drop moment that we cannot afford to miss. Here, as in the epistle to the Romans, Paul develops his idea that those promises made to Abraham were *not* made to the Jews as a race or a people. Rather, those promises were made to Christ, and anyone who is in Christ qualifies as an heir who also shares in those same promises.

So, going back to what Paul said in Romans 9:6–8, we see that:

> "…they are not all Israel who are descended from Israel; nor are they all children because they are Abraham's descendants… That is, it is not the children of the flesh who are children of God, but the children of the promise are regarded as descendants."

The significance for Christians here is phenomenal. It means that because Christ is the fulfillment of those promises made to Abraham, we are now considered the children of God, and the children of Abraham, and therefore the children of the promises made to Israel. Or, to put it another way, anyone who is in Christ is considered Israel.

> HERE, AS IN THE EPISTLE TO THE ROMANS, PAUL DEVELOPS HIS IDEA THAT THOSE PROMISES MADE TO ABRAHAM WERE *NOT* MADE TO THE JEWS AS A RACE OR A PEOPLE. RATHER, THOSE PROMISES WERE MADE TO CHRIST, AND ANYONE WHO IS IN CHRIST QUALIFIES AS AN HEIR WHO ALSO SHARES IN THOSE SAME PROMISES.

As we said earlier, it really does matter how we define Israel. If we really hope to understand what's going on in the New Testament in terms of fulfillment of promises and Biblical prophecy, we really need to be clear on this one thing: Israel does not refer to the average Jewish individual. It refers specifically and uniquely to anyone who is in Christ.

What John Nelson Darby did, after his fall from the horse all those years ago, was to forget (or overlook) everything Paul said about the identity of Israel and the definition of a Jew, in the spiritual sense. By reverting things back to a pre-Christian definition of Israel and Jew, Darby started to believe that there were dozens of promises made to the Jews and the nation of Israel that were never fulfilled. This, he assumed, must mean that there are still unfulfilled prophecies about the Jewish people and the nation of Israel that must still need to come to pass before the Second Coming of Christ can take place.

As tragic as this misunderstanding may be in terms of understanding Biblical prophecy and End Times theology, it is even more disturbing to consider the implications that follow such reasoning. Why? Because the bulk of Christian theology developed by the Apostles throughout the New Testament is based on how Christ is the fulfillment of all of those Old Testament promises made to Israel. So, if we now take a step backwards and deny this has happened, we are essentially replacing Christ with an ethnic people group that ultimately rejects Jesus as their Messiah and denies the resurrection.

Ironically, one of the names used by Dispensationalists to describe non-Dispensational theology is "Replacement Theology", because they say we are replacing Israel with the Church. However, an even greater tragedy occurs whenever someone dares to replace Christ and all that he has done with anything or anyone else.

Again, it's not that the Church has "replaced" Israel at all. Rather, as the Apostle Paul and Jesus both affirm, Israel is and always has been defined as those who are inwardly born of God. So, the promises made to Abraham were always intended to refer to Christ, and now that Christ has come and fulfilled those promises, we who are in Christ are now also identified with him, and with the essence of what it means to be Israel. So, if anything, one might call this "Fulfillment Theology" since it hinges on the fact that Jesus has fulfilled those promises and now everyone who is in Christ has become the Israel of God.

FURTHER STUDY

One of the pillars of Dispensationalism is the idea that Israel and the Church are two separate and distinct groups of people. But, is that what the New Testament affirms? Let's take a look.

According to Charles C. Ryrie, "A dispensationalist keeps Israel and the church distinct", adding "..this is probably the most basic theological test of whether or not a person is a dispensationalist."[7]

So, for Dispensational Theology to be taken seriously, we must establish whether or not the Scriptures affirm the distinction between Israel and the Church. As we've already seen, Paul goes out of his way to establish the identity of Israel as all who are in Christ. But, is there any evidence to suggest that Israel and the Church are somehow distinct in the eyes of God? Are the Dispensationalists on to something we seem to have overlooked? Or are they the ones who have misread the scriptures?

To answer this, I'd like to quote a lengthy response to this question from author and Bible scholar, Ken Gentry who says:

> "In dispensationalism's two-peoples-of-God theology they must hold that God (1) distinguishes Jew and Gentile and (2) that he does so permanently (at least in history, though many carry the distinction into eternity). How are these observations fatal to the system? And in light of our study in Ephesians, how do we see that problem in Paul's epistle? We must first ask the question regarding the dispensationalist's assumption: Who makes up the people known as 'Israel'? The obvious answer is 'Jews,' the genetic offspring of Abraham. But then the question arises in the debate: Does God establish a new entity in redemptive-history which also includes Jews? The answer is: Yes. The church of Jesus Christ. In fact, it was established in the very context and on the foundation of Israel. *Indeed, Paul notes very clearly and forcefully that God merges Jew and Gentile into one body, which we now call the church.* He even encourages the Gentiles with the knowledge that they are now included among God's people

and are partakers of their blessings. They are not separate and distinct from Israel but are adopted into her.

"Note Ephesians 2:11–19: 'Therefore remember, that *formerly you, the Gentiles in the flesh,* who are called 'Uncircumcision' by the so-called 'Circumcision,' which is performed in the flesh by human hands—remember that *you were at that time separate from Christ, excluded from the commonwealth of Israel, and strangers to the covenants of promise,* having no hope and without God in the world. *But now in Christ Jesus you who formerly were far off have been brought near* by the blood of Christ. For He Himself is our peace, *who made both groups into one,* and broke down the barrier of the dividing wall, by abolishing in His flesh the enmity, which is the Law of commandments contained in ordinances, that *in Himself He might make the two into one new man,* thus establishing peace, and might reconcile them *both in one body* to God through the cross, by it having put to death the enmity. And He came and preached peace to you who were far away, and peace to those who were near; for through Him we both have our access in one Spirit to the Father. So then you are no longer strangers and aliens, but you are fellow citizens with the saints, and are of God's household.'

"Note very carefully what Paul states and how it contradicts the notion of a distinction between Jew and Gentile, between Israel and the church."[8] [emphasis mine]

As Gentry points out for us, the epistle from Paul to the Ephesians completely decimates the notion that God has drawn a distinction between Israel and the Church and goes out of his way to establish the fact that God has merged these two separate groups into one.

For example, Paul says that the Gentiles were "formerly... at that

AS GENTRY POINTS OUT FOR US, THE EPISTLE FROM PAUL TO THE EPHESIANS COMPLETELY DECIMATES THE NOTION THAT GOD HAS DRAWN A DISTINCTION BETWEEN ISRAEL AND THE CHURCH AND GOES OUT OF HIS WAY TO ESTABLISH THE FACT THAT GOD HAS MERGED THESE TWO SEPARATE GROUPS INTO ONE.

time... excluded from the commonwealth of Israel, and strangers to the covenants of promise", (Eph.2:12). This was their prior condition. However, this has all changed, because "...now in Christ you who formerly were far off have been brought near" (Eph. 2:19). This indicates a change in condition that Paul further explains this way: "[Christ] has made both groups into one, and broke down the barrier of the dividing wall" (Eph 2:14)

So, in Christ both groups—Israel and the Church—are now made into one. This should remind us of the passage in Galatians where Paul affirms:

> "So in Christ Jesus you are all children of God through faith, for all of you who were baptized into Christ have clothed yourselves with Christ. *There is neither Jew nor Gentile*, neither slave nor free, nor is there male and female, *for you are all one in Christ Jesus*." (Gal. 3:26-27) [emphasis mine]

Therefore, what we see is that God not only does *not* draw any distinction between Israel and the Church, He has gone out of His way to unite both of these in Christ and make them into one new entity.

Some Dispensationalists might suggest that this passage in Ephesians speaks of a temporary peace between Israel and the Church, but such a notion is entirely impossible according to what Paul says here. As Gentry points out:

> "If you read the passage carefully... you will note that the whole tenor of Paul's theological observation is that: Jew and Gentile have been merged into one body forever. There is absolutely nothing in the passage that hints at or even will allow that this union into one new body is temporary. Everything about the passage demands that this merger be permanent. Read it again and try to find any intimation that this merger of Jew and Gentile is just temporary until the Rapture or the millennium or whatever. You will find nothing that leads to that conclusion and everything that militates against it.

"...Christ did not preach a temporary 'truce' between Jew and Gentile, but a permanent 'peace.' He did not suspend the enmity between Jew and Gentile for a while but 'put to death the enmity.' He did not bring the two peoples together for a time (nor even for a time, times, and half a time) but he permanently created a new man. Dispensationalism's theology requires that ultimately we must separate what God has joined together. It allows the rebuilding of the dividing wall." [9]

So, according to what we read in Ephesians, Romans and Galatians, the identity of Israel is defined as "those who are in Christ", not merely those who are born into a Jewish household, or those who have been circumcised. Instead, the Body of Christ is where the Israel of God lives and breathes. The two are not separate or distinct, but have now—because of the work of Christ—become inseparable and synonymous in the eyes of God.

This means that Christ has fulfilled the promises made to Israel, and that the Body of Christ (the Church) is the ongoing reality and testimony of this fulfillment. It also means that there are no unfulfilled prophecies still waiting to be accomplished. Christ said he came to fulfill the Law and the Prophets at the very beginning of his ministry, (Matt. 5:17–18). Later, he affirmed that he had indeed accomplished this mission, both before the cross (John 17:4) and during the crucifixion itself (John 19:30).

Therefore, when Dispensationalists base their theology on the assumption that Israel and the Church are distinct and separate, the entire thing falls apart once we realize that this assumption has no foundation whatsoever to stand upon. It simply isn't true.

There is one other pillar of Dispensationalism that we need to examine and that is the unique End Times Narrative developed by Darby and promoted by Futurist Bible teachers around the globe. This is probably the most relevant teaching we must explore in this book, since it is the source for all of the Last Days hype and hoopla that we are forced to endure today.

THE SIGNS OF THE END

One of the main outcomes of Darby's theology has been the tendency to apply current events to Biblical prophecies in the hopes of determining the date of the Second Coming of Christ and the End of the World. One clear example of this comes when we recognize that the earliest failed prophecy about the return of Christ came in 1844—just 14 years after Darby's theology had become known—and this trend has continued ever since.

ONE OF THE MAIN OUTCOMES OF DARBY'S THEOLOGY HAS BEEN THE TENDENCY TO APPLY CURRENT EVENTS TO BIBLICAL PROPHECIES IN THE HOPES OF DETERMINING THE DATE OF THE SECOND COMING OF CHRIST AND THE END OF THE WORLD.

Prior to 1830, when John Nelson Darby first introduced his Dispensational Theology, the concept of a Pre-Tribulation Rapture was practically unheard of. Yes, there were some obscure references to this idea floating around, but none that were taken seriously until Darby popularized them.

For example, there are two early Church Fathers—Hippolytus and Irenaeus—who both made mention of a future end times scenario that sounds much like what Darby suggested in 1830. Hippolytus (170–235 AD) was one of the most important second century Christian theologians. He was a disciple of Irenaeus (130–202 AD), a Greek Bishop who helped to define Christian orthodoxy in his day. Both of them make statements about the End Times that are worth examination.

Irenaeus wrote that:

"Once this Anti-Christ has devastated everything in the world, he will reign for 3 years and 6 months and sit in the Temple in

Jerusalem. And then the LORD will come from heaven in the clouds."[10]

Hippolytus, who studied under Irenaeus, also taught something similar when he said:

"[The Anti-Christi will] rebuild the city of Jerusalem, and restore the sanctuary."[11]

Adherents of Darby's Dispensational Theology will often point to these two quotes as proof that their End Times scenario—involving the necessity for the rebuilding of the Temple in Jerusalem and the rise of an Anti-Christ figure who will sit in the Temple prior to the second coming of Christ—was embraced by the early Church.

So, while it is true that Hippolytus and Irenaeus both believed in the rise of a future Anti-Christ and the rebuilding of the Jewish Temple prior to the return of Christ, this view was not popular by any stretch of the imagination. Quite frankly, the view belongs primarily to Irenaeus himself and was merely passed along to his student, Hippolytus who repeated the teaching. What we see is that we have no other record of anyone else in the second century who held this view or affirmed it. None prior to this, nor afterwards, embraced such a view other than these two men. This should tell us something. Apparently, all the other Church Fathers rejected such notions as unfounded in Scripture.

It wasn't until Jesuit writers Francisco Ribera (1537–1591) and Manuel Lacunza (1731–1801) proposed their Futurist views of the Second Coming of Christ over a thousand years later that these ideas came around again. It's worth noting that the Catholic Church at the time banned these writings and condemned them as heretical. Why? Because these ideas were not embraced by the Christian Church. They were strange, sensational and seen as against the grain of Christian theology to that point.

Still, it is interesting to note that there is some evidence that John Nelson Darby may have read at least some of the writings of Manuel Lacunza in his studies. Perhaps this is where at least some his ideas originally came from.

There were a handful of other pastors and theologians prior to Darby's eschatology who espoused ideas similar to his. People like John Owen (1616–1683)[12], John Gill (1697–1771)[13], and even Jonathan Edwards (1703–1758)[14] published statements about their belief that the Jewish people would return to their homeland prior to the return of Christ. However, it wasn't until Darby solidified these ideas in 1830 that notions such as this took a deep hold on the Christian Church.

At any rate, such Futurist ideas of an Anti-Christ appearing and the rebuilding of a Jewish Temple in Jerusalem prior to the coming of Christ were quite rare before they became popularized by Darby. He may not have invented these ideas himself, but he certainly gave them a renewed credibility in the Christian Church when he began teaching them as part of his Dispensational Theology.

END TIMES NARRATIVE

Darby's eschatology is what this book is written to explain and expose. His Futurist theology is marked by several key teachings which we will examine one at a time. These are:

- Daniel's 70th week is a future event

- The Olivet Discourse (Matt. 24, Luke 21 Mark 13) is about future events

- The Abomination of Desolation hasn't happened

- The Jewish temple must be rebuilt before Christ returns

- The Jewish animal sacrifice must resume

- The Anti-Christ must appear before the rapture

- Revelation is about what will happen in the end times

- All prophetic Scriptures are literal (not spiritual)

- The day of the LORD is about the future return of Christ

Let's take these one by one and see if what Darby and the Dispensationalists teach about these things is indeed true, or if there have been some misunderstandings or confusion regarding the nature of these scriptures and the intention of these prophecies.

CHAPTER 4

SEVENTY WEEKS OF DANIEL

"And thus Christ became King of the Jews, reigning in Jerusalem in the fulfillment of the seven weeks [of Daniel]... And Christ our Lord, 'the Holy of Holies,' having come and fulfilled the vision and the prophecy, was anointed in His flesh by the Holy Spirit of His Father. In those 'sixty and two weeks,' as the prophet said, and 'in the one week,' was He Lord."

— CLEMENT OF ALEXANDRIA[1]

In the Old Testament book of Daniel, there are several prophetic dreams and visions given to the prophet. Some of his final visions and dreams deal with the coming of the Messiah, the specific timing of when he would appear, and about when "the power of the holy people [the Jews] will be finally broken." (Dan. 12:7)

Much of what Darby and other Dispensationalists get wrong is in how they read and interpret Daniel's 70 Weeks prophecy found in chapter 9, starting in verse 20 and going through verse 27. Let's look at the passage itself before we examine several key statements in this prophecy that need to be understood.

"Seventy 'sevens' [or 'weeks'] are decreed for your people and your holy city to finish transgression, to put an end to sin, to atone for

wickedness, to bring in everlasting righteousness, to seal up vision and prophecy and to anoint the most holy."

"Know and understand this: *from the issuing of the decree to restore and rebuild Jerusalem until the Anointed One* [Messiah], *the ruler, comes, there will be seven 'sevens'* [weeks], *and sixty-two 'sevens'* [weeks]. It will be rebuilt with streets and a trench, but in times of trouble. *After the sixty-two 'sevens'* [weeks], *the Anointed One will be cut off and will have nothing,* [or, 'cut off, but not for himself'].

"The *people of the ruler who will come will destroy the city and the sanctuary.* The end will come like a flood: War will continue until the end, and desolations have been decreed. *He* [The Messiah] *will confirm a covenant with many for one 'seven'* [week]. *In the middle of the 'seven'* [week] *he will put an end to sacrifice and offering.* And on a wing of *the temple,* he will set up *an abomination that causes desolation,* until the end that is decreed is poured out on him [or 'on it']. (Dan. 9:24-27) [emphasis mine]

Before we get into how we should understand this passage, it's probably a good idea to understand a little of how Dispensationalists interpret this section of the Bible.

"According to some of the most popular "prophecy teachers," Dan 9:24–27 is the biblical prediction of the antichrist signing a seven-year covenant treaty with the newly established Israel, which initiates the tribulation depicted in Revelation 6–16. The biblical reference on which the signing of the treaty is based is found in Dan 9:27… But how can Dan 9:27 be used to explain the initiation of the tribulation as described in Revelation 6–16?

"Practitioners of premillennial dispensational hermeneutics pay little attention to the historical context from which a biblical book comes. In addition, they frequently pull individual verses out of context and weave them together with biblical verses from very different biblical contexts to create a new text, which they then interpret. Add to these methodological approaches the hermeneutics of the Israel—Church divide (one of the foundational beliefs of premillennial dispensationalism), a literal reading of prophetic texts, as well as the belief that all prophecies point to the second coming of Jesus, and the end result is an historically flat and one-dimensional interpretation of the Bible."[2]

So, our goal here is to take a fresh look at this passage, without viewing it through a Dispensational lens to see what the passage might actually be about.

Most Dispensationalists will agree that the first 69 "weeks" of this prophecy deal specifically with the timing of the coming of the Messiah. Let's explain what these "weeks" are all about before we go any further.

SO, IF WE WANT TO KNOW WHEN THE MESSIAH WILL APPEAR, WE HAVE TO START COUNTING "FROM THE ISSUING OF THE DECREE TO REBUILD JERUSALEM." BUT THIS IS WHERE THINGS GET TRICKY. BECAUSE THERE ARE 3 DIFFERENT DECREES WE COULD START FROM.

The "seventy sevens" or "weeks" spoken of here are symbolic. Each "week" corresponds to seventy "weeks" of years, or 490 years. So, if we want to know when the Messiah will appear, we have to start counting "from the issuing of the decree to rebuild Jerusalem." But this is where things get tricky. Because there are 3 different decrees we could start from:

- King Artexerxes gave a decree allowing Nehemiah to go and rebuild the walls of Jerusalem in 445 BC.

- King Artexerxes gave another proclamation in 457 BC.

- King Cyrus gave a proclamation for the Jews to return and build the temple in 539 BC.

So, which decree do we start counting from? In some ways, I'm not sure it matters very much. I've seen Bible Scholars who start from either of these 3 decrees and end up either at the birth of Jesus, the triumphal entry of Jesus on Palm Sunday, or the

Crucifixion of Christ, or even the stoning of Stephen in Acts 7:54.

What does matter is this: From either of those 3 decrees if we count forward 490 years we end up with the timeframe of the ministry of Jesus and several other events that Daniel mentions would take place at the end of the age. As noted earlier, Dispensationalists and non-Dispensationalists agree on this point. It's not something disputed by either perspective, so for the sake of our study let's move on to the sections where we do see things differently.

THE REASON THIS DETAIL IS SIGNIFICANT IS BECAUSE DARBY AND OTHER DISPENSATIONALISTS TODAY TEND TO READ THE PORTION ABOUT PUTTING "AN END TO SACRIFICE AN OFFERING" AND CONFIRMING "A COVENANT WITH MANY" AS IF IT WERE REFERRING TO THE ANTI-CHRIST RATHER THAN TO JESUS.

ANOINTED ONE CUT OFF

Looking once more at the passage in Daniel 9, we see the prophecy about the Anointed One (the Messiah) being cut off:

> "After the sixty-two 'sevens' [weeks], the Anointed One will be cut off and will have nothing, [or, 'cut off, but not for himself']." (v.26)

In what way was the Messiah "cut off"? Well, quite obviously when he was betrayed and crucified on a Roman cross. But more importantly, Daniel's prophecy also tells us when this will take place: "In the middle of the 'seven' [week] he will put an end to sacrifice and offering" and this is after the Messiah "[confirms] a covenant with many for one 'seven' [week]."

The reason this detail is significant is because Darby and other Dispensationalists today tend to read the portion about putting "an end to sacrifice and offering" and confirming "a covenant with many" as if it were referring to the Anti-Christ rather than to Jesus.

First, let's ask why they do this. Well, other than that this is how many of them have been trained to read this passage, the hiccup tends to be the fact that Daniel makes a reference to *"the people of the ruler who will come will destroy the city and the sanctuary"* just before this passage. This verse makes them think that everything that comes after it is about "the ruler who will come" and not the Messiah.

Perhaps this is an honest mistake, but if we look closely at the passage, we'll notice a few things. First, that the reference is to "the *people* of the ruler", not the ruler himself. See that? Daniel says that it will be the "people of the ruler who will come [to] destroy the city and the sanctuary", not the Anti-Christ. Second, there is not one single reference to the Anti-Christ anywhere in this passage. Just look. I'll wait. See? Nothing. The entire thing is about the Messiah who will come, not about the Anti-Christ.

So, while Daniel does make an aside about "the people of the ruler" destroying the city of Jerusalem and the Temple, the subject of this passage is still primarily talking about the Messiah to come.

HOW JESUS FULFILLS DANIEL 9

Another important thing to note here is that Jesus actually *does* fulfill everything in the passage that Dispensationalists want to attribute to the unnamed Anti-Christ. For example, Jesus does indeed "confirm a covenant with many" in the upper room when he raises the cup and proclaims the New Covenant in his blood. (Luke 22:20) Jesus also "put an end to sacrifice and offering" in several ways: First, by literally ripping the veil in the Temple from top to bottom at his crucifixion (Matt. 27:51) which would have made it impossible to continue the daily sacrifices, and second by fulfilling the shadow of animal sacrifice when he offered himself as the ultimate sacrifice upon the cross (Heb. 7:27).

Jesus also did these things when he was "cut off... in the middle of the week" because if a week equals seven years, then the middle of that time frame would be three and a half years, and Jesus's ministry was ended after three and a half years when he was "cut off" by being arrested, beaten and crucified. How do we know this is how long the ministry of Jesus lasted? Because in Luke 3:23 we're told that Jesus began his ministry just after John the Baptist showed up during the 15th year of the reign of Tiberius Caesar, which was the year 26 AD. The crucifixion is said to have taken place in the spring of 30 AD. Furthermore, in John's Gospel we're told that Jesus attended three different Passover Festivals. (See John 2:13, 6:4 and 11:55–57) All of this indicates a ministry that spanned a three-year period, so the three-and-a-half-year time frame mentioned in Daniel fits this timeline.

Now, we should also admit that the daily sacrifice and offering was also ultimately brought to an end when the Romans surrounded Jerusalem and destroyed the city and the Temple in 70 AD. So, there is a double-fulfillment if you like: Jesus fulfills the requirement as far as God is concerned because Jesus was "the Lamb of God who takes away the sins of the world" (See John 1:29; 36), and of course when the Romans destroyed the Temple in 70 AD the ritual of animal sacrifices—which had continued after the crucifixion of Jesus—were finally ended for good. But, as far as the fulfillment of this prophecy is concerned, when Jesus offered himself upon the cross as the true lamb of God, this was the "end of sacrifices."

As the author of Hebrews makes plain:

"…we have been made holy through the sacrifice of the body of Jesus Christ once for all." (Heb. 10:10)

Because,

"Day after day every priest stands and performs his religious duties; again and again he offers the same sacrifices, which can never take away sins. But when this priest [Jesus Christ] had offered for all time one sacrifice for sins, he sat down at the right hand of God, and since that time he waits for his enemies to be made his footstool. For by one sacrifice he has made perfect forever those who are being made holy." (Heb. 10:11-14)

And now, after what Jesus suffered on the cross,

"…sacrifice for sin is no longer necessary." (Hebrews 10:18)

We might also take a moment at this time to point out that any future rebuilding of the Temple in Jerusalem at this point would not only be in complete violation of everything we read in Hebrews about what Jesus accomplished by fulfilling the shadow of sacrifice on the cross, it would also be completely superfluous since those shadows of the Old Temple system have now been fully realized in Christ. Today, the Church is now the Temple of God where we, as members of the Priesthood of All Believers offer ourselves as living sacrifices to God, forever. (See 1 Cor. 3:17; 6:19, Eph. 2:19–22, 1 Peter 2:4–5; 9–10)[3]

SEVENTIETH WEEK POSTPONED?

Another strange quirk of the Dispensationalist view is that they insert a massive gap between the 69th and 70th weeks of Daniel's prophecy. Why do they do this? Because they need that final week of the prophecy to refer to some future event. Otherwise, the entire passage is about something that already happened in our past and it's not actually about anything yet to come.

As author and Bible scholar LeAnne Snow Flesher explains:

"...the numbers do not add up perfectly for a premillennial dispensational interpretation of Daniel; [therefore] dispensationalists fill the gap by suggesting that the divine 'counter' stopped just before the death of Jesus, with seven years still left to go. The remaining seven-year period is what they call the tribulation... The only way one can make any kind of sense of this is through the hermeneutics of dispensationalism.

"Why in the world would the divine counter stop? Even worse, according to the full doctrine of premillennial dispensationalism, the dispensation of the church began on the day of Pentecost (Acts 2), which took place sometime after the death of Jesus. Why would the divine counter stop just before the death of Jesus? In order to fit it all in—the dispensation of the church, the dispensation following the rapture, and the seven-year tribulation—the clock must stop ticking. In essence, premillennial dispensationalism claims a special time for a special group, i.e., the true church. This special group will then be raptured before the tribulation to become the bride of Christ, after which the unfulfilled promises to Israel will finally be fulfilled in the new dispensation. Premillennial dispensationalists claim Dan 9:23–27 is a very important text because many of the events predicted by this group flow out of this moment; this moment when the divine clock stopped ticking."[4]

So, in essence, Dispensationalists claim the prophetic clock has stopped because it has to stop if their theology is going to make any sense. As arbitrary as that may sound, it's pretty much the only reasoning offered as to why we should assume that a prophecy like Daniel 9, built upon the premise of a specific number of weeks adding up to 490 years, should somehow have an additional insertion of a pause that takes over 2,000 years (and counting) to fulfill.

One might wonder, if the intention all along was to have this final week take place over 2,000 years later, then why not just say this? Why package the entire thing into a metaphorical Seventy Weeks but then fail to mention that the last part isn't actually going to take place in that specific time frame? What's more, if the prophecy includes events that will not be fulfilled until much, much later, then why not have that final week presented all by itself? Wouldn't that make much more sense? And, finally, if there is a gap of over 2,000 years, shouldn't there be some indication of this gap somewhere in the prophecy itself?

In spite of the fact that this theory creates more questions than it answers, Dispensational Futurists have no problem adding it into their story. And for some reason, Christians haven't had much problem with this practice since it was first proposed by Darby in 1830. There's a gap. Why? There just has to be. How long is the gap? Over 2,000 years long. How do you know that? We just know. Ok, then.

THE ABOMINATION OF DESOLATION (PART 1)

One of the most misunderstood terms in Biblical prophecy is this reference to the "abomination that causes desolation" in Daniel 9:24-27. Here it is again for our reference:

> "...and on a wing of *the temple,* he will set up *an abomination that causes desolation,* until the end that is decreed is poured out on him [or 'on it']"

This is where things may get a little tricky. Hopefully we can follow along without too much confusion.

There are several suggestions for what this verse could be speaking of. No doubt you've heard that this is a reference to when Antiochus desecrated the Temple by sacrificing a pig on the altar around 160 BC. The problem with his theory is that it occurs way before the Messiah shows up, so it's unlikely to be what the author had in mind here.

There is a reference as we mentioned earlier to "the people of the ruler who will come to destroy the city and the sanctuary" (v.26), and this has to refer to the Romans who, in 70 AD actually did surround the city of Jerusalem and destroy the Jewish Temple. Therefore, the reference to the "abomination that causes desolation" can't refer to Antiochus since he was the King of the Seleucid Empire, not the Roman Empire, and also because Antiochus came much too soon to have fulfilled something that should have taken place in the 70th week of Daniel's prophecy.

Another wrinkle in all of this has to do with the English translation of Daniel in our modern Bibles. As I've written about extensively and provided examples for in my book *Jesus Unbound: Liberating the Word of God from the Bible*, our version of the scriptures are often wildly different from what the actual Greek or Hebrew texts say. Sometimes these changes are accidental, but more often than not these changes are intentionally made to obscure the true meaning. Usually these altered passages deal with the role of women in the Church, or with Church hierarchy, or are translated in such a way as to make us believe the scriptures have something to say about homosexuality, even though the word "homosexual" never appeared in any English translation of the Bible until 1946.[5]

So, in this passage we're unfortunately also at the mercy of a fairly poor English translation of this text. I'm not suggesting that the translation here is intentionally obscure, although given what we've seen in other examples, it wouldn't surprise me. However, if we go to the King James Version of this passage in Daniel 9 the verse is slightly different:

> "And he shall confirm the covenant with many for one week: and in the midst of the week he shall cause the sacrifice and the oblation to cease, and for the overspreading of abominations he shall make it desolate, even until the consummation, and that determined shall be poured upon the desolate." (Dan. 9:27)

Perhaps we may find this translation isn't much clearer than the NIV version above it, but what it does help us to see is that it is not necessarily "he" who "will set up an abomination that causes desolation"—as if the Messiah is the one creating the abomination. Here, the action seems to be more that the Messiah will *cause the sacrifice and the oblation to cease"*—something Jesus obviously did when he fulfilled the shadow of Temple sacrifice upon the cross—and the rest seems to be more of a natural outcome of all of this.

This conclusion is supported by the fact that neither the Septuagint nor the Hebrew Interlinear mention any "he" in relation to the abomination and simply state that *"an abomination of desolations will be..."* So, we may logically conclude that because the sacrifice has ended, the abominations and desolations that follow are merely the result of this fulfillment.

Keep in mind, Jesus came to warn his people of a coming destruction of Jerusalem. His intention was *not* that they would be destroyed but that they would listen to him and escape this fate. It was because "God so loved the world that he sent his only begotten son that whoever placed their trust in him [the Messiah] would not perish but have life." (John 3:16) So, God's intention is that, through the testimony and ministry of Jesus, the Jewish people would *avoid* the destruction that was to come. Jesus offers them a new path that would lead them to life. However, since the majority of his people rejected him and his message, they continued moving in the direction they were already going in, and this led to the destruction that Jesus had warned them about.

KEEP IN MIND, JESUS CAME TO WARN HIS PEOPLE OF A COMING DESTRUCTION OF JERUSALEM. HIS INTENTION WAS NOT THAT THEY WOULD BE DESTROYED BUT THAT THEY WOULD LISTEN TO HIM AND ESCAPE THIS FATE.

Therefore, Jesus is vindicated and proven right when the things he predicted came to pass in 70 AD. We'll talk more about this later when we explore the words of Jesus in the Olivet Discourse. But, for now let's agree that the abomination that causes desolation is the fruit that came from rejecting the words of Jesus and not something that Jesus personally made happen.

Another thing we notice from the King James version of this passage above is that we've lost the reference to "...*on the wing of the temple*" where this abomination is supposed to take place. Instead, that same section is translated as "...*and in the midst of the week he shall cause the sacrifice and the oblation to cease...*" which is a pretty huge change. No mention of "wing" or "temple" at all. Instead, a mention of the time-frame being in the "midst of the week" which we know is at the end of three and a half years when Jesus is crucified.

So, what's going on here? Why do so many different English translations of this passage disagree about the terms and specific wording to use?

Well, we should probably make note of the fact that this text is especially difficult to parse because the Hebrew and Septuagint texts they were translated from aren't in agreement. For example, in the Hebrew Interlinear version, the term "Temple" doesn't appear, but the word "wing" does appear. In the Septuagint version of this passage, the word "wing" isn't there, but the word for "Temple" is.[6]

So, getting to the actual meaning of the text is more than challenging, especially when you're not even totally sure which version is accurate. Even in the New Revised Standard Version (NRSV) this text includes a notation that says the meaning for the Hebrew word "place" used in this verse is uncertain. Welcome to the exciting world of Biblical translation.

My friend Katy Valentine, who has a PhD in Biblical studies, says this about the passage in Daniel:

> "Hebrew is such a supple language, and this is a long, long sentence and thought, hence convoluted with a lot of translations. [However], using 'temple' is strange and in my opinion incorrect. The most common way to say 'temple' in Hebrew is "house of the LORD" and that's not in this verse. It's the word for 'wing' that some translations render as 'temple'."[7]

So, different translations emphasize different aspects of this prophecy in Daniel 9:27, and they can't seem to agree on whether the words "place", "temple", or "wing" should be there, or not, and if so, what they exactly mean.

In addition, the translation of this passage that say *"he will set up an abomination…"* can't be correct because neither the Hebrew Interlinear nor the Septuagint include a reference to "he" and instead say *"an abomination of desolations will be…"*, without attributing it directly to either the Messiah or the Anti-Christ.

But the main things we need to recognize are simply that:

- Jesus made a covenant with us in the upper room

- Jesus put an end to the daily sacrifice by offering himself as the final sacrifice on the cross, and

- The abomination that causes desolation is the end result of everything that happens.

Still, we haven't actually discovered what *"the abomination that causes desolation"* is talking about yet. What is it? How do we know it already happened if we're not even sure what it's referring to?

If we want a clue about what this phrase is in reference to, we actually need to turn to the Olivet Discourse—found in Matt.

24, Mark 13, and Luke 21—where Jesus not only makes reference to Daniel's prophecy but actually tells us *exactly* what it refers to.

CHAPTER 5

JESUS THE PROPHET

"I am not a believer, but I must confess as a historian that this penniless preacher from Nazareth is irrevocably the very center of history. Jesus Christ is easily the most dominant figure in all history."
— H.G. WELLS[1]

According to Dispensationalist eschatology, Jesus tells us about the events leading up to his second coming, the rapture and the end of the world in what's known as the Olivet Discourse found in three of our four Gospels. But, is that what Jesus is talking about here? Let's see.

If we look at the Olivet Discourse given by Jesus as it is recorded in the first three Gospel records, we'll notice that the entire conversation starts as he and his disciples are leaving the Temple. This is true in all three versions, as chronicled in Matthew, Mark and Luke.

Notice how each of the Gospels starts off this section:

"Jesus left the temple and was going away, when his disciples came to point out to him the buildings of the temple. But he answered them, 'You see all these, do you not? Truly, I say to you, there will not be left here one stone upon another that will not be thrown down.'" (Matt. 24:1–2)

"And as he came out of the temple, one of his disciples said to him, "Look, Teacher, what wonderful stones and what wonderful buildings!" And Jesus said to him, "Do you see these great buildings? There will not be left here one stone upon another that will not be thrown down." (Mark 13:1–2)

"And while some were speaking of the temple, how it was adorned with noble stones and offerings, he said, 'As for these things that you see, the days will come when there will not be left here one stone upon another that will not be thrown down.'" (Luke 21:5–6)

So, as the disciples stop to marvel at how amazing the Temple is, Jesus uses this as an opportunity to share some rather shocking information with them: *This Temple will be completely destroyed and not one stone will be left upon the other.* As you might imagine, this greatly upsets and troubles the disciples and in each case their response is the same:

"As he sat on the Mount of Olives, the disciples came to him privately, saying, 'Tell us, when will these things be, and what will be the sign of your coming and of the end of the age?'" (Matt. 24:3)

"And as he sat on the Mount of Olives opposite the temple, Peter and James and John and Andrew asked him privately, 'Tell us, when will these things be, and what will be the sign when all these things are about to be accomplished?'" (Mark 13:3–4)

"And they asked him, 'Teacher, when will these things be, and what will be the sign when these things are about to take place?'" (Luke 21:7)

Here, the response from the disciples in each case is nearly identical. They want to know: "When will these things happen?" and "What will be the sign when this is about to be accomplished?" Notice that it is only in Matthew that the disciples ask, "What will the sign of your coming be and of the end of the age?" This is significant for a few reasons. First, because even though Matthew is the only place where it records the disciples asking about the sign of Jesus's coming and the end of the age, the responses given by Jesus are the exact same in all three Gospels. So, this tells us that everything Jesus talks about in each of these three versions of the Olivet Discourse are all primarily talking about the destruction of the Temple. The additional questions about the signs of his coming and the end of the age are both directly tied to the same event in question: the destruction of the Temple. How do we know this? Because if Matthew intended to answer that second question about his coming and the end of the age as a separate

SO, THIS TELLS US THAT EVERYTHING JESUS TALKS ABOUT IN EACH OF THESE THREE VERSIONS OF THE OLIVET DISCOURSE ARE ALL PRIMARILY TALKING ABOUT THE DESTRUCTION OF THE TEMPLE.

event, then we should expect to see additional signs given to answer that extra question. But since all three versions of the Olivet Discourse contain the same signs, we can reasonably conclude that all three are talking about the same thing.

Here's another reason we know that all three versions of the Olivet Discourse are about the same thing: Because the end of the age and the coming of Jesus referenced in Matthew are fulfilled when the Temple is destroyed. Wait. They are? I can almost hear some of you asking. Yes, they are. Because the *end of the age* is not the *end of the world* as we have been told to understand it. In the book of Daniel we were told about a time that was coming where "the power of the holy people [the Jews] will be finally broken." (Dan. 12:7) This is a large part of what the Seventy Weeks prophecy is also about. This might help to refresh your memory:

> "*Seventy 'sevens'* [or 'weeks'] *are decreed for your people and your holy city to finish transgression, to put an end to sin, to atone for*

*wickedness, to bring in everlasting righteousness, to seal up vision
and prophecy and to anoint the most holy."*

"….The *people of the ruler who will come will destroy the city and
the sanctuary. The end will come like a flood...*" (Dan. 9:24–27)
[emphasis mine]

In this passage, we're told that there are Seventy Weeks
"decreed for your people and your holy city…" and this is a
final countdown for the Jewish people and for Jerusalem and the
Temple. What is being prophesied here is the "end of the age"
for the Jewish people. It's also why we read that "the people of
the ruler who will come will destroy the city [Jerusalem] and
the sanctuary [the Temple]" and that "the end will come like a
flood." What end? The end of the Jewish age.

So, let's try to get a few things straight before we dive into
much more of this. The Olivet Discourse is a prophecy from
Jesus about the coming destruction of the Temple in Jerusalem.
The Disciples are shocked by this. They want to know what the
signs will be of this destruction, and also what the signs will be
of the end of the age. *Because they understand that this is what
Jesus is referring to.*

But, what about where they ask about "the sign of your coming?" Isn't that about the Second Coming of Jesus? Well, yes and
no. Not in the sense that we have always been told to understand
the Return of Jesus at least. But, yes,
in the sense that the coming of Jesus
being referred to is in relation to the
destruction of the Temple and the
end of the age.

**WHAT OFTEN CONFUSES
US IS THAT WE'VE BEEN
TRAINED TO THINK OF
"THE RAPTURE" WHENEVER
WE HEAR JESUS TALK
ABOUT "THE SIGN OF [HIS]
COMING", AND THAT'S
NOT THE SAME THING.**

What often confuses us is that
we've been trained to think of "the
rapture" whenever we hear Jesus talk

about "the sign of [his] coming", and that's not the same thing. There are numerous examples of where the coming of God, or of Jesus, is not a positive event but a sign of judgement. For example, in Revelation we read where Jesus addresses the Seven Churches and to each one he gives a warning: "Therefore repent. If not, I will come to you soon and war against them with the sword of my mouth" (Rev. 2:16) and that if they do not repent he will "come to them and remove [their] lampstand." (Rev. 2:5)

In each of these examples, the promised "coming" Jesus speaks of is not a happy occasion. It's a warning. This is exactly the same sort of "coming" referred to by the disciples in the Olivet Discourse.

We might also want to go ahead and point out that there are other examples where Jesus mentions that many will see him "coming on the clouds," and that when he uses this phrase we should understand what this is in reference to. And it's not a literal appearance of Jesus in the sky at his Second Coming.

Here's what I mean: In the Old Testament scriptures we have numerous examples where it is said that God would "come in the clouds" and these references were not literal—God did not actually appear in the sky or ride on a cloud like a pony—and these were also not about the end of the world as we know it, but a form of Apocalyptic Hyperbole where metaphors are used to describe events using overly-descriptive language.

Here are some examples from the Old Testament where "coming in the clouds" is not a reference to an actual physical appearance of God (or Jesus) in the sky, but is a poetic reference to an invading army coming against a city or a nation in the form of judgement:

> "Behold, the LORD is riding on a swift cloud and comes to Egypt; and the idols of Egypt will tremble at his presence, and the heart of the Egyptians will melt within them." (Isaiah 19:1)

In this passage, the Assyrian army attacks Egypt and it is described as "the Lord riding on a swift cloud" as He "comes to Egypt", however just as the idols did not actually tremble in fear and the hearts of the Egyptians did not literally melt, neither did God actually ride on a cloud in the sky.[2] This is Apocalyptic Hyperbole. Here's another reference to God "coming in the clouds":

> "[God] makes the clouds his chariot; he rides on the wings of the wind; he makes his messengers winds, his ministers a flaming fire." (Ps. 104:3)

Here is another reference to God using "clouds" as "his chariot" and "riding on the wings of the wind" as symbols of God's judgement. These are never literal references but used poetically to describe God's power in hyperbolic terms. And here's just one more reference to drive our point home:

> "Behold, [God] comes up like clouds; his chariots like the whirlwind; his horses are swifter than eagles—woe to us, for we are ruined!" (Jer. 4:13)

THE IMAGERY OF GOD COMING IN THE CLOUDS IS AN OFTEN-USED BIBLICAL REFERENCE TO GOD'S JUDGMENT AGAINST A CITY OR A NATION.

I don't want us to get bogged down with examples here, so hopefully I've made my point. The imagery of God coming in the clouds is an often-used Biblical reference to God's judgment against a city or a nation. It is fulfilled not when people look up and see God riding on clouds in the sky, but when the prophesied destruction of that city or nation is fulfilled when invading armies overtake them as predicted.[3]

So, when Jesus predicts the destruction of the Temple at the start of the Olivet Discourse, the disciples question about the "coming" of Jesus and the "end of the age" is synonymous with this same event. They are one and the same. The "coming" referenced is in relation to the destruction, not to the rapture.

Now, let's get back to how Jesus answers the questions about when these things will be and what the signs of his coming and the end of the age will be. Here's how Jesus explains it in all three versions of the Olivet Discourse:

> "And Jesus answered them, "See that no one leads you astray. For many will come in my name, saying, 'I am the Christ,' and they will lead many astray. And you will hear of wars and rumors of wars. See that you are not alarmed, for this must take place, but the end is not yet. For nation will rise against nation, and kingdom against kingdom, and there will be famines and earthquakes in various places. All these are but the beginning of the birth pains." (Matt. 24:4–8; Mark 13: 5-8; Luke 21: 8–11)

All three Gospels record this text, nearly verbatim so there's no need to show you all of them side-by-side. But what we do want to point out is that he's telling these disciples not to be led astray by others who will came later claiming to be the Messiah. Why? Because there were several people who came before Jesus claiming this, and we know historically that there were many who came later claiming the same thing. But please note: This happened in the first century. It happened in Jerusalem. The Jewish people at this time were desperate to find a Messiah—any Messiah—who was willing to lead them in an armed rebellion against the Romans and re-establish the throne of David over Jerusalem and all of Palestine. After 70 AD there weren't so many Messiah's rising up to lead Jewish rebellions. Why? Because the end of the age had already taken place. (Note: The siege of Masada was the final Jewish rebellion in 73 AD but it failed horribly.)

We might also note that when Jesus warns the Disciples that there will be "wars and rumors of wars" before the end of the age and the destruction of the temple, this was an unusual and surprising statement. Why? Because at this time in history, everyone who lived under Roman rule enjoyed what was known as the *Pax Romana.* That is, Rome had enforced peace by the edge of the sword and conquered all their largest enemies so that there was no longer any threat of war or any rumors of wars when Jesus said this. However, soon afterwards there were several wars and conflicts leading right up to the destruction of the temple in 70 AD. For example, the Roman historian Tacitus records an increasing numbers of insurrections and battles breaking out all over the Roman Empire, up until the death of Nero in 68 AD.[4] And Josephus, a Jewish historian who recorded Roman history during the time of Christ and afterwards also reports that there were so many wars and civil disturbances leading up to the events in 70 AD that he didn't bother to record all of them.

This is also another clue as to why Jesus really isn't speaking about anything in the future, beyond 70 AD because ever since that time wars have been as commonplace as rain and sunrise. Truly, the sign given to the disciples that there would be wars and rumors of war only makes sense to those living in Jerusalem between 40 AD and 70 AD.

It is also true that between the time when Jesus made his prophecy on the Mount of Olives and the eventual destruction of Jerusalem in 70 AD, there were many earthquakes and an outbreak of famine. For example, the book of Acts references an earthquake occurring soon after the Ascension of Christ (See Acts 16:26) and historically we know that, prior to 70 AD, there were earthquakes in Crete, Smyrna, Miletus, Chios, Samos, Laodicea, Hierapolis, Colosse, Campania, Rome, and Judea.[5]

We also find famines recorded in Acts 11:28 and in Romans 8:35, exactly as Jesus predicted, and contemporary historians such as Suetonius, Tacitus and Josephus all record famines lead-ing up to 70 AD.[6]

So, all of these signs that Jesus refers to in this first section of the Olivet Discourse actually were fulfilled just as he predicted prior to the destruction of the temple in 70 AD.

I know, we haven't gotten to the Abomination of Desolation yet. But, we're almost there. I promise. Just one last section to look at before we get to it, and it's worth exploring, believe me.

In this next section, Jesus provides more details about what his disciples can expect to see as "signs" that the "end of the age" is at-hand when the temple is destroyed. Once again, all three versions of the Olivet Discourse record nearly the same state-ments with a few exceptions. I've emphasized a few key words and statements across all three Gospels that I want you to notice:

"Then they will deliver *you* up to tribulation and put *you* to death, and *you* will be hated by all nations for my name's sake. And then many will fall away and betray one another and hate one another. And many false prophets will arise and lead many astray. And because lawlessness will be increased, the love of many will grow cold. But the one who endures to the end will be saved. *And this gospel of the kingdom will be proclaimed throughout the whole world as a testimony to all nations, and then the end will come.*" (Matt. 24: 9–14) [emphasis mine]

"But be on *your* guard. For they will deliver *you* over to councils, and *you will be beaten in synagogues,* and *you* will stand before governors and kings for my sake, to bear witness before them. *And the gospel must first be proclaimed to all nations.* And when they bring *you* to trial and deliver *you* over, do not be anxious beforehand what *you* are to say, but say whatever is given *you* in that hour, for it is not *you* who speak, but the Holy Spirit. And brother will deliver brother over to death, and the father his child, and children will rise against parents and have them put to death. And *you* will be hated by all for my name's sake. But the one who endures to the end will be saved." (Mark 13:9–13) [emphasis mine]

"But before all this they will lay their hands on *you* and persecute *you, delivering you up to the synagogues* and prisons, and *you* will be brought before kings and governors for my name's sake. This will be *your* opportunity to bear witness. Settle it therefore in your minds not to meditate beforehand how to answer, for I will give *you* a mouth and wisdom, which none of *your* adversaries will be able to withstand or contradict. *You* will be delivered up even by parents and brothers and relatives and friends, and *some of you* they will put to death. *You* will be hated by all for my name's sake. But not a hair of *your* head will perish. By *your* endurance *you* will gain *your* lives." (Luke 21: 12–19) [emphasis mine]

I admit it may seem petty, but I have emphasized every instance where Jesus uses the term "you" in this section. Why? Because we must remember that the disciples asked him a question about the temple which he is now in the process of answering. He is talking to them, not to us. He's telling them what the signs are that they need to be watching for so they'll know that the time is near for the temple to be destroyed and for the end of the age to come. This is our entire context. We cannot make this about us. Especially since you'll also notice that I bolded the parts where Jesus warns them that they will be "delivered up to the synagogues." Do you ever worry that you'll be brought up to the synagogues? Is that one of your End Times scenarios? Do you imagine that Christians in the Last Days will be escorted to appear before the Jewish authorities? Probably not. That detail seems to have been lost in the shuffle for most Dispensational Futurists. But it wasn't lost on Jesus or his disciples. Because

DO YOU EVER WORRY THAT YOU'LL BE BROUGHT UP TO THE SYNAGOGUES? IS THAT ONE OF YOUR END TIMES SCENARIOS? DO YOU IMAGINE THAT CHRISTIANS IN THE LAST DAYS WILL BE ESCORTED TO APPEAR BEFORE THE JEWISH AUTHORITIES? PROBABLY NOT.

they understood that *they* would be taken before the synagogues in their community, and beaten, and accused of blasphemy for preaching about Jesus and His Kingdom. Again, this entire discourse is for them, not for us, and it is about something that was about to happen in their future, not in ours.

Of course, we also need to address this little part about how "...this gospel of the kingdom will be proclaimed throughout the whole world as a testimony to all nations, and then the end will come," (Matt. 24:19) and that "...the gospel must first be proclaimed to all nations." (Mark 13:10) as a sign of these things coming to pass. Dispensationalism teaches that the end of the age cannot possibly have happened because the Gospel has *not* been preached to the whole world, or to all the nations. Therefore, there must still be something left unfulfilled. Right?

Wrong. At least, according to what we read in the rest of the New Testament, anyway. Let's start by looking at the various prophecies concerning specifically how far the Gospel needs to be preached before "the end shall come", shall we?

"...this Gospel of the Kingdom shall be preached *in all the world* [oikumene]...then the end shall come" (Matt. 24:14) [emphasis mine]

"And the Gospel must first be preached among *all the nations* [ethnos]..." (Mark 13:10) [emphasis mine]

"Go into *all the world* [kosmos] and preach the Gospel *to every creature* [kitisis]." (Mark 16:15) [emphasis mine]

"...and you shall be witnesses in Jerusalem, and all Judea and Samaria, and to *the end of the earth* [ge]." (Acts. 1:8) [emphasis mine]

Now, let's see if we can find any evidence in the New Testament that the Gospel has—or has not been—preached to all the world (*oikumene* and *kosmos*), the nations (*ethnos*), the end of the earth (*ge*) and to every creature (*kitisis*). And if we look, what we'll see is that the Apostle Paul seems to believe that the Gospel of the Kingdom *was* preached in all the world. He says as much in 4 different places:

> "But they have not all *obeyed the gospel*... But I ask, have they not heard? Indeed they have, for '*Their voice has gone out to all the earth* [ge], and their words *to the ends of the world* [oikumene]" (Rom. 10:16–18) [emphasis mine]

> "...according to my gospel and the preaching of Jesus Christ, according to the revelation of the mystery that was kept secret for long ages but has now been disclosed and through the prophetic writings *has been made known to all nations* [ethnos], according to the command of the eternal God, to bring about the obedience of faith..." (Rom. 16:25-26) [emphasis mine]

> "...*the gospel,* which has come to you, as indeed *in the whole world* [kosmos] it is bearing fruit and increasing..." (Col. 1:5–6) [emphasis mine]

> "...not shifting from the hope of the gospel that you heard, *which has been proclaimed to every creature* [kitisis] under heaven..." (Col. 1:23) [emphasis mine]

So, according to Paul, the Gospel *was* preached "in the whole world", "in all creation", "to all the earth", "to the ends of the world" and was "made known to all nations." He even makes sure to use the same three Greek words from the original prophecy in his statements that they have been fulfilled so we have no doubt. Now, does that mean that the Rapture is soon to take place? No, but it *does* mean that everything necessary for the "end of the age" and the "destruction of the Temple" that Jesus predicted was fulfilled during the New Testament era and came to pass in 70 AD.

Are you ready for the part about the Abomination of Desolation? I imagine so. You've been quite patient so far and

I want you to know I appreciate that, very much. So, without further ado, let's jump into it.

THE ABOMINATION OF DESOLATION (PART 2)

When we do the comparison between Matthew, Mark and Luke we notice something very interesting. First, that Matthew and Mark use almost the exact same language regarding the Abomination of Desolation:

> "So *when you see the abomination of desolation spoken of by the prophet Daniel, standing in the holy place (let the reader understand),* then let those who are in Judea flee to the mountains. Let the one who is on the housetop not go down to take what is in his house, and let the one who is in the field not turn back to take his cloak. And alas for women who are pregnant and for those who are nursing infants in those days! Pray that your flight may not be in winter or on a Sabbath." (Matt. 24: 15–20; Mark 13:14–18) [emphasis mine]

Other than the addition of the remark in Matthew about the Sabbath, both Mark and Matthew are nearly identical. But, when we look at the version in Luke something astounding happens. Watch this:

> "But *when you see Jerusalem surrounded by armies, then know that its desolation has come near.* Then let those who are in Judea flee to the mountains, and let those who are inside the city depart, and let not those who are out in the country enter it, for these are days of vengeance, to fulfill all that is written. Alas for women who are pregnant and for those who are nursing infants in those days!" (Luke 21:20–23) [emphasis mine]

Wow. Did you see that? The "Abomination of Desolation spoken of by the prophet Daniel" bit is now replaced by an entirely new phrase: "when you see Jerusalem surrounded by armies, then you know its desolation is near." So, according to

Jesus, what is the abomination of desolation about? It's about when the Roman armies surround Jerusalem and prepare to destroy the Temple.

Now, we might wonder why Matthew and Mark don't come right out and say it the way Luke does. One reason might be because Matthew was writing to primarily Jewish audiences. We know this for several reasons. For example, whenever Jesus refers to the "Kingdom of God" in Luke, Matthew refers to it as "the Kingdom of Heaven", because Jewish audiences would not want to refer to God by name, out of respect. Therefore, the term gets softened for their benefit. Referring to "heaven" is one way that the authors of Scripture will often refer to God without actually using the term. And in this example, perhaps Matthew and Mark both felt confident that their Jewish Christian audience would require nothing more than the reference to the Prophet Daniel's mention of the abomination of desolation, whereas Luke's audience would need much more of an explanation to understand what this was referring to. Therefore, Luke opts to cut to the chase and explain it straight away.

> SO, ACCORDING TO JESUS, WHAT IS THE ABOMINATION OF DESOLATION ABOUT? IT'S ABOUT WHEN THE ROMAN ARMIES SURROUND JERUSALEM AND PREPARE TO DESTROY THE TEMPLE.

Whatever their reasons, we can be thankful that the three Gospel writers conspired in this way to reveal to us what the abomination of desolation is actually all about. It's about the fulfillment of the prophecy by Daniel that the end of the age would come when the Messiah was cut off after his three and a half year ministry culminated in the declaration of a covenant and his death which ended the daily sacrifice and set up the abomination of desolation which was the destruction of the Temple, bringing about the end of the age.

This might be a good time to catch your breath. We're about to power through the rest of the Olivet Discourse. There's a lot to cover so I hope you're ready for it. Here goes.

THE GREAT TRIBULATION

According to John Nelson Darby and the Dispensational Futurists—which sounds like a great name for a band—the "Tribulation" is something that Christians will suffer once the Anti-Christ rises to power and forces everyone to take the Mark of the Beast. But as we shall soon see, Jesus mentions nothing about the Anti-Christ rising up in this discourse, and makes no mention about anyone being forced to take a mark on their head or the hand. We'll have to address those questions in another chapter, but for now I want you to notice that the Dispensational narrative of End Time events involves playing Mister Potato Head with various elements found all over the Bible and mashing them together to concoct a version of the Last Days that isn't actually there.

In other words, someone has to first tell you the Dispensational version of the End Times story. After that, they can take you to several verses scattered all over the Bible and use this one to prove one thing and this other verse to prove something else. But if you simply read the Bible from beginning to end you'd never connect those dots yourself. Those connections just aren't there. But Darby and the Dispensationalists need them to connect, so they force these concepts together to create a grand story about the End Times that is only loosely based on Scripture or fact.

Having said that, let's get back to what Jesus has to say to his disciples about the signs of the end of the age and the destruction of the Temple in Jerusalem, shall we?

Jesus continues:

"For then *there will be great tribulation, such as has not been from the beginning of the world until now, no, and never will be.* And if those days had not been cut short, no human being would be saved. But for the sake of the elect those days will be cut short. Then if anyone says to you, 'Look, here is the Christ!' or 'There he is!' do not believe it. *For false christs and false prophets will arise and perform great signs and wonders, so as to lead astray, if possible, even the elect.* See, I have told you beforehand. So, if they say to you, 'Look, he is in the wilderness,' do not go out. If they say, 'Look, he is in the inner rooms,' do not believe it. *For as the lightning comes from the east and shines as far as the west, so will be the coming of the Son of Man. Wherever the corpse is, there the vultures will gather.*" (Matt. 24:21–28) [emphasis mine]

Note: Mark 13:22 is identical to the above, except for this last section referencing "lightning" and "the corpse." Also, it's at this point that Luke begins to diverge from the parallels found in Matthew and Mark. Luke, therefore, does not contain any specific references to the "great tribulation", "false christs and false prophets", or the "corpse" and "vultures" verse.

In this section, only Matthew and Mark mention several key elements such as the "great tribulation", the false christs and prophets to come, and the final section about "lightning" and the cryptic statement about corpses and vultures. So, let's deal with these specifically before we move on to the next sections where the three Gospels start to line up again.

THE GREAT TRIBULATION

Here, Matthew and Mark talk about the "great tribulation"—which is a reference to what Jesus has already warned them about when those who are his disciples would be arrested, beaten, brought before the synagogues and persecuted for preaching about the Good News of the Kingdom of God. Again, Jesus is answering his disciples' questions about the events leading up to the destruction of the Temple. And this is indeed what we know actually happened, according to what we read in the book of Acts, and from Church history. Those who followed Christ prior to the destruction of the Temple in 70 AD were persecuted. They were brought before the Jewish leaders and beaten. They were told not to preach in the name of Jesus. They were thrown in jail. All of these things are recorded in the book of Acts, and we know that these things were fulfilled as Jesus predicted. So, whenever anyone asks if you think Christians will go through the Great Tribulation, you can tell them that they already did, and it was horrible.

Now, I understand that what trips up a lot of Dispensationalists is the fact that Jesus says that this tribulation will be "…such as has not been from the beginning of the world until now, no, and never will be" and this sounds like it's something that has to be the absolute worst thing that has ever— or will ever—happen to anyone, ever. So, since we've seen a lot of human cruelty and horrific accounts of genocide over the last few thousand years, we're tempted to say that, whatever this "great tribulation" is, it must be something worse than the Holocaust, and the Killing Fields of the Khmer Rouge, and the massacre of the Native Americans all rolled together in order to qualify as something that "has not been seen from the beginning of the world until now, no, and never will be."(v.21)

THIS IS WHERE I NEED TO STOP AND REMIND YOU ABOUT HOW THE JEWISH PROPHETS USED APOCALYPTIC HYPERBOLE ALL THROUGHOUT THE BIBLE TO OVERSTATE THE INTENSITY OF SOMETHING IN ORDER TO AMPLIFY THEIR POINT AND DRIVE HOME THEIR WARNING TO THOSE WHO WERE LISTENING.

This is where I need to stop and remind you about how the Jewish prophets used Apocalyptic Hyperbole all throughout the Bible to overstate the intensity of something in order to amplify their point and drive home their warning to those who were listening.

Here are a few examples of the very same hyperbole used by other prophets throughout Scripture:

> "And because of all your abominations *I will do with you what I have never yet done, and the like of which I will never do again.*" (Ezekiel 5:9) [emphasis mine]

This verse is about the impending destruction of Jerusalem in 586 BC. It uses the exact same phrases to describe something that is so horrible that such a thing has never and will never be done again. Jesus applied the same language to the impending destruction of Jerusalem in 70 AD. Both events, in the common hyperbole of the day, are spoken of as if they were each uniquely horrendous, but this is simply for emphasis.

The same language is used to describe a locust plague:

> "The locusts came up over all the land of Egypt and settled on the whole country of Egypt, such a dense swarm of *locusts as had never been before, nor ever will be again.*" (Exodus 10:14) [emphasis mine]

> "Like blackness there is spread upon the mountains a great and powerful people; their like *has never been before, nor will be again after them through the years of all generations.*" (Joel 2:2) [emphasis mine]

What's especially interesting about these two verses is that both are describing a plague of locusts, and both claim to be the worst ever experienced in the history of the world. But, of course, they can't both be the absolute worst locust plague ever sent, can they? Of course not. The point is not to determine which the worst of all time was. The point is that the prophets are both employing Apocalyptic Hyperbole to stress to their audience that something really, really bad is about to happen and they really need to take what's being said as seriously as possible.

In Daniel 9:12, we have yet another example of this same language being used:

> "You have fulfilled the words spoken against us and against our rulers by bringing on us great disaster. Under the whole heaven *nothing has ever been done like what has been done to Jerusalem.*" [emphasis mine]

Once again, Apocalyptic Hyperbole is being used to speak about an event in absolute terms which are not intended to literally qualify as the "worst thing that has ever happened in the history of our planet", but instead serve to emphasize that something is indeed quite horrible and significant.

So, when Jesus talks about a "great tribulation, *such as has not been from the beginning of the world until now, no, and never will be…*" we should pay attention to the fact that he's using Apocalyptic Hyperbole, and not try to force his statements to be literally true. His audience, the Jewish disciples, would have been quite familiar with this prophetic language and understood it in context.

We might also mention that this "great tribulation" also includes the destruction of Jerusalem and the Temple, since one leads directly to the other. When we explore the details of what happened during the tragic events of 70 AD, you'll start to see why the 40 years-long persecution of Christians and the ultimate destruction of Jerusalem's Temple qualifies as the "Great Tribulation" that Jesus is referring to here.

The second thing we want to examine in this section of the Olivet Discourse is the prediction that many "…false christs and false prophets will arise and perform great signs and wonders, so as to lead astray, if possible, even the elect." (Matt. 24:24) We know from an historical standpoint that there were many failed Messiah's who rose up during this time frame. In fact, one of those is mentioned in the book of Acts, when Paul is beaten and dragged out of the Temple:

> "Are you not the Egyptian, then, who recently stirred up a revolt and led the four thousand men of the Assassins out into the wilderness?" (Acts 21:38)

The Egyptian mentioned here was one of several "Messiahs" who rallied support, gathered an army and attempted to lead an insurrection against the Roman Empire. Like all of them, they failed and were put to the sword, or crucified for their rebellion. In fact, it was this continual

IN FACT, IT WAS THIS CONTINUAL AND PERSISTENT DESIRE FOR REVOLUTION THAT EVENTUALLY LED TO THE DESTRUCTION OF JERUSALEM AND THE TEMPLE BY THE ROMANS.

and persistent desire for revolution that eventually led to the destruction of Jerusalem and the Temple by the Romans. If the Jewish people "had known the things that make for peace" (Luke 19:42), as Jesus attempted to show them, this destruction wouldn't have taken place. But, because their hearts were steadfastly set on overthrowing their oppressors by force, they lived by the sword, and died by it, too, just as Jesus had warned them. (See Matt. 26:52)

The last thing mentioned by Matthew in this section of the Olivet Discourse is this:

> "For as the lightning comes from the east and shines as far as the west, so will be the coming of the Son of Man. Wherever the corpse is, there the vultures will gather." (Matt 24:27–28)

Dispensationalists see this as proof that Jesus is referring to his literal Second Coming in the sky. But as we've already seen earlier, references to "coming in the clouds" or even to God "coming" in this context—which is the Judgment of Jerusalem and the destruction of the Temple—is never a good thing. Nor is it ever a literal description of God arriving in the sky for all to see. This verse, as in every other example we've already examined, is simply telling us that this "coming of the Son of Man" will be swift and unmistakable to those who are in Jerusalem to see it take place.

The final sentence in this passage used to stump me for many years. I couldn't make sense of it no matter how hard I tried, and my study Bible was no help either. It wasn't until someone pointed out to me that the symbol used by the Roman Army was the Eagle and it was emblazoned on their battle shields and on their breastplates and even carried by flag-bearers when they marched into battle. So, once you realize this and then you find out that the Greek word of "vultures" and the Greek word of "eagles" is the exact same word, you can start to understand what Jesus is referring to when he says:

"Wherever the corpse is, there the vultures [or 'eagles'] will gather." (v.28)

Quite simply, the "corpse" is Jerusalem and the "vultures" or "eagles" are the Roman Army which surrounds the city and prepares to devour it whole.

THE TIMES OF THE GENTILES

In the Gospel of Luke, while it does not contain this section we've just explored, it does contain a reference we probably need to examine before we move on to where all three Gospels realign. This is where Luke's Gospel records a statement from Jesus which says:

"They will fall by the edge of the sword and be led captive among all nations, and Jerusalem will be trampled underfoot by the Gentiles, until the times of the Gentiles are fulfilled." (Luke 21:24)

This verse is mostly significant because of what it says about when "the times of the Gentiles are fulfilled." This is because, to the Dispensationalists, this verse is pretty much their only thread to base their idea of a rebuilt Jerusalem and Temple on. So, as you can imagine, it's pretty important to them. And you may be asking yourself, "where does it say that there will be a rebuilt Jerusalem or Temple in this passage?", and the answer would be that if you squint a little when you read it, you'll notice that it says "Jerusalem will be trampled underfoot by the Gentiles, *until the times* of the Gentiles *are fulfilled*", and therefore once the times of the Gentiles are finally fulfilled, that must mean that Jerusalem won't be trampled underfoot by them anymore. That leaves open the possibility that, one day when that time is up, Jerusalem and the Temple will rise again.

Of course, you and I know that in 1948 the Jewish people were relocated to the Middle East, and Israel became a nation once more. This seems like a fulfillment of prophecy, except that there's really nothing prophesied here about any of that. What we have is an "until", but that hardly qualifies as anything specifically predicted about a return to Jerusalem or the rebuilding of the Jewish Temple, which hasn't happened as of the writing of this book.

Still, it does seem like an impressive event that Israel was restored as a nation, doesn't it? And Dispensationalists do credit John Nelson Darby for predicting such a thing in 1830 when he proposed his unique theological views of the End Times. But what we should keep in mind is that the people who were most instrumental in the creation of the restored nation of Israel were Christian Zionists who believed Darby's eschatology and did everything they could to make it come to pass. In other words, if Darby hadn't made such a prediction and hinged his theology on the necessity for the restoration of Israel and eventually the rebuilding of a Jewish Temple in Jerusalem, no one would have thought to try to make it happen. Darby's prediction is what set these events in motion, and to this day we are seeing events take place in the Middle East that are driven by Darby's eschatology as Christian Zionists work hard to fulfill their own prophecies and usher in the Second Coming of Jesus.

As Dr. Ninan Koshy explains it for us:

"Christian Zionism began as an ally of British imperialism, legitimizing colonial expansion. The unique and controversial pre-millennial eschatology had a seminal influence both on the establishment and the ongoing support for the modern state of Israel. Key 19th century British political figures came under its influence leading them to lend support to the Jewish Zionist movement begun by Theodore Herzel. The theology of Darby, Way and their followers influenced a number of prominent English politicians and may have made British Foreign Secretary Arthur Balfour more receptive to the idea of creating a Jewish national home in Palestine. David Lloyd-George was perhaps even more predisposed to the Zionist ideology than Balfour. British imperial designs were undoubtedly the primary political force in drawing influential British politicians to support the Zionist project because of their Christian Zionist background."[7]

So, if you're not familiar with the history of how Israel became a nation in 1948, it was something set into motion when British Foreign Secretary Arthur Balfour (mentioned above) issued the "Balfour Declaration" on November 2, 1917, which was really not much more than a few paragraphs written to Walther Rothschild, a leading figure in the British Jewish community, expressing support for the notion of establishing a Jewish homeland in Palestine.

At the time, Palestine was part of the crumbling Ottoman Empire which had been at war with the

DARBY'S PREDICTION IS WHAT SET THESE EVENTS IN MOTION, AND TO THIS DAY WE ARE SEEING EVENTS TAKE PLACE IN THE MIDDLE EAST THAT ARE DRIVEN BY DARBY'S ESCHATOLOGY AS CHRISTIAN ZIONISTS WORK HARD TO FULFILL THEIR OWN PROPHECIES AND USHER IN THE SECOND COMING OF JESUS.

British Empire since 1914. This declaration was made without consulting any of the 650,000 inhabitants of Palestine, and even though Britain had no legal claim to the territory at the time, the plan was set in motion.

As one historian explains it:

"In fact, the story of the Balfour Declaration began 20 years earlier. In 1897, the Zionist movement held its inaugural congress in Basel, Switzerland, with the aim of establishing a Jewish state. The common nationalist thinking in those days was that every people needed a homeland. Since the Zionists considered Jews a people without a homeland, a homeland had to be found. And the most logical place for it, according to the Zionists, was Palestine."[8]

We should also understand that the eventual establishment of the nation of Israel was something that had to be forced into being as it was in direct contradiction to various declarations and agreements in place at the time.

"The Balfour Declaration appeared to be in stark contradiction to American President Woodrow Wilson's 'Fourteen Points', a statement of principles for peace which became the blueprint for post-war peace negotiations, and the joint declaration issued by the British and French governments on 8 November 1918, in which they assured the peoples of Syria, Palestine and Mesopotamia that Allied policy was aimed at 'the setting of national governments and administrations that shall derive their authority from the free exercise of the initiative and choice of the indigenous population'.

"The Balfour Declaration was also in contradiction to the Covenant of the League of Nations, especially the articles about self-determination and, in particular, paragraph 4 of Article 22, which states that: '...subject to the rendering of administrative advice and assistance by a Mandatory until such time as they are able to stand alone. The wishes of these communities must be a principal consideration in the selection of the Mandatory.'

"In reality, the wishes of 'these communities' did not play a role in British thinking... As Balfour put it bluntly in a memorandum to the British government in August 1919: 'In Palestine we do not propose even to go through the form of consulting the wishes of the present inhabitants of the country, though the American Commission has been going through the form of asking what they are. The four great powers are committed to Zionism. And Zionism, be it right or wrong, good or bad, is rooted in age-long traditions, in present needs, in future hopes, of far profounder importance than the desires and prejudices of the 700,000 Arabs who now inhabit that ancient land.'" [9]

So, without the direct influence of religious and political Zionists, the nation of Israel as we now know it would never have been established at all. Not that there's anything wrong necessarily with the Jewish people being restored into their homeland, but without these events we wouldn't have the current Middle East peace crisis we see today where Palestinian Christians and Muslims are in daily conflict with the state of Israel over this disputed territory, leading to hundreds of thousands of deaths and endless violent conflicts that rage in this region on a near-daily basis.

What's more, this Dispensational Futurism is still driving foreign policy in the Middle East today. Quite recently, our President, under the guiding hand of our Dispensational Evangelical Vice President, Mike Pence, declared Jerusalem as the capital of Israel on Dec. 6, 2017. This decision, which was denounced by the Pope, dozens of European leaders, and even a former director of the C.I.A. as a "reckless" move which would *damage U.S. interests in the Middle East for years to come and make the region more volatile,*[10] makes no sense whatsoever from a purely political perspective. But, it makes all kinds of sense if you believe that such things must take place in order to speed up the Second Coming of Christ.

As reported in the article by the *New York Times*, "Mr. Trump's promise to move the embassy appealed to evangelical voters and pro-Israel American Jews..."[11] So, the only reason for making such disastrous foreign policy decisions like this one is simply this: Because it fits the Dispensational End Times scenario of the Christian Church.

All of this took place because Darby's eschatology influenced Christian thinking in 1830, and those who embraced it began to coerce history towards an end times scenario they believed must take place so that Jesus can return. This mindset leads us toward an eventual conflict where millions of Jewish people will be slaughtered in order to provide Jesus with a green light to come back and rescue us from this fallen world, and utterly destroy it in the process.

ALL OF THIS TOOK PLACE BECAUSE DARBY'S ESCHATOLOGY INFLUENCED CHRISTIAN THINKING IN 1830, AND THOSE WHO EMBRACED IT BEGAN TO COERCE HISTORY TOWARDS AN END TIMES SCENARIO THEY BELIEVED MUST TAKE PLACE SO THAT JESUS CAN RETURN.

Keep in mind, the verse that partially supports this vision is one that merely says "Jerusalem will be trampled underfoot until the times of the Gentiles are fulfilled." (Luke 21:24) Does this prove that Jerusalem must be reestablished as the capital of Israel? Does it prove the Jewish Temple must be rebuilt? Or, does it merely suggest that the trampling underfoot of Jerusalem will come to an end once the time of the Gentiles is over?

THE TEMPLE IN JERUSALEM REBUILT?

Of course, there are other reasons why Dispensational Futurists believe the Temple in Jerusalem must be rebuilt. As we've already seen, because they believe Daniel's Seventy Weeks prophecy is about a future event, the logical conclusion is that the Temple must exist in order for the Anti-Christ to show up and stop the daily sacrifices (again). Even though Daniel's prophecy doesn't mention any Anti-Christ figure, the End Times narrative established by Darby says that the Temple needs to be built one last time, so that the events in Daniel (which have already been fulfilled by Christ) can be fulfilled one final time.

But, if we go back and look at that prophecy in Daniel, it doesn't say that the end result of all of these things—the ending of the daily sacrifice and the abomination of desolation—will result in the second coming of Christ. No such reference exists. What we see, instead, is that once these events happen "the end that is decreed is poured out." Meaning, it's the end of the age, not the triumphant return of Jesus in the sky.

If we want to find a picture of Jesus returning in the clouds, we have to turn back to the Olivet Discourse, where we do see "the Son of Man coming on the clouds of the sky, with power and great glory." (Matt. 24:30) But notice what we don't see in the Olivet Discourse is this: The description of the Temple being destroyed. Now, isn't that odd? The entire dialog starts when Jesus tells the disciples the Temple is going to be thrown down to the ground and not one stone will be left upon another. So, everything that follows is about answering their questions about when these things will take place and what the sign of this "coming" will be. If so, then, why don't we see Jesus conclude his teaching by saying, "And then the Temple will be destroyed"? Here's why: Because everything that Jesus says in the Olivet Discourse IS a description of what will happen leading up to the ultimate destruction of the Temple. So, when Jesus describes his "coming on the clouds of the sky with power and great glory", it's the very same type of "coming in the clouds" we've already seen in other Apocalyptic visions throughout the Old Testament. The audience here already understands what this "coming in power and great glory" is about: it's the destruction of the city and the nation in question.

THE END TIMES TEMPLE

Still, it's worth mentioning that Dispensationalists and some orthodox Jewish Rabbis believe that the Temple in Jerusalem must be rebuilt before the Messiah will come. For those of the Jewish faith, the rebuilding of the Temple marks the sign of the coming of the Messiah for the first time, and for Dispensationalists it would mark the second coming of Christ. But, they both require this rebuilding of the Temple in Jerusalem prior to this Messiah coming/returning because they both don't recognize how Jesus has already fulfilled these prophecies. Dispensationalists don't recognize that Jesus is the one in Daniel 9 who "confirms a covenant with many for one seven" and who will "put an end to the daily sacrifice" (Dan. 9:27), and the Jewish Rabbis don't recognize that Jesus already established the End Times Temple the first time he arrived on the scene.

> FOR JEWS, ONE OF THE MAIN THINGS THEIR MESSIAH MUST DO IS TO ESTABLISH A TEMPLE IN JERUSALEM THAT WILL ENDURE FOREVER. THIS IS ONE OF THE REASONS WHY JEWISH PEOPLE DO NOT ACCEPT JESUS AS THEIR MESSIAH, BECAUSE THEY DO NOT BELIEVE HE ESTABLISHED SUCH A TEMPLE.

Here's what I mean: For Jews, one of the main things their Messiah must do is to establish a Temple in Jerusalem that will endure forever. This is one of the reasons why Jewish people do not accept Jesus as their Messiah, because they do not believe he established such a temple. In fact, when Jesus arrived on the scene, there was a wonderful temple already standing in Jerusalem, and if anything, Jesus prophesied the destruction of that temple, he did not build one that would endure until the end of time. Or did he?

See, if you're expecting Jesus to build a physical temple that lasts forever, you're out of luck. However, what we do see is that Jesus established the true "Temple of God" which was first of all his own body (See John 2:21), and then secondly, the Church which is often referred to throughout the New Testament as the Temple of God. For example:

> "Don't you know that *you yourselves are God's temple* and that God's Spirit lives in you?" (1 Cor. 3:16) [emphasis mine]

> "Do you not know that *your body is a temple of the Holy Spirit*, who is in you, whom you have received from God? You are not your own." (1 Cor. 6:19) [emphasis mine]

> "What agreement is there between *the temple of God* and idols? *For we are the temple of the living God.* As God has said: "I will live with them and walk among them, and I will be their God, and they will be my people." (2 Cor. 6:16) [emphasis mine]

> "Consequently, you are no longer foreigners and aliens, but fellow citizens with God's people and members of God's household, built on the foundation of the apostles and prophets, with Christ Jesus himself as the chief cornerstone. *In him the whole building is joined together and rises to become a holy temple in the LORD. And in him you too are being built together to become a dwelling in which God lives by his Spirit.*" (Eph. 2:19–22) [emphasis mine]

We might also want to remember that when Stephen was stoned to death in the book of Acts it was largely because he reminded his Jewish brothers and sisters that "God does not live in temples made by human hands" and that God said "Heaven is my throne and earth is my footstool, where is the house you will build for me?" (Acts 7:48–49) To those listening, this was a blasphemy against their own Temple building, but it was in fulfillment of God's promise to David in 2 Samuel 7:11 to build a house for David through one of his own sons:

> "I will send one of your descendants, one who will come from you. I will establish his kingdom. He will build a house for my name, and I will establish the throne of his kingdom forever. I will be his Father, and he will be my Son… Your royal house will remain in my presence forever. Your throne will be established forever.'" (2 Sam. 7:12–16)

So, when Jesus shows up on the scene, there is already a temple in Jerusalem. But that's not the temple that he was prophesied to build. No, the temple that Jesus the Messiah was coming to build was one not made by human hands but by Spiritual hands that crafted a dwelling place made out of living stones, which is all about us, the Bride of Christ and the Temple of the Living God here on Earth which will endure for eternity.

THEREFORE, THE MESSIAH *DID* BUILD A TEMPLE, AND IT *WILL* ENDURE FOREVER. THERE IS NO LONGER ANY NEED FOR ANY OTHER TEMPLE TO BE BUILT.

Therefore, the Messiah *did* build a Temple, and it *will* endure forever. There is no longer any need for any other Temple to be built. There's no prophecy that a new one will be built in Jerusalem in Scripture, and if one day someone does build one, it will be in direct defiance of the Temple already established by God Himself and by the Messiah that He has sent. We are the End Times Temple of God:

> "As you come to him, the living Stone—rejected by men but chosen by God and precious to him—you also, like living stones, are being built into a spiritual house to be a holy priesthood, offering spiritual sacrifices acceptable to God through Jesus Christ." (1 Peter 2:4–5)

> "But you are a chosen people, a royal priesthood, a holy nation, a people belonging to God, that you may declare the praises of him who called you out of darkness into his wonderful light.

Once you were not a people, but now you are the people of God; once you had not received mercy, but now you have received mercy." (1 Peter 2:9–10)

THE OLIVET DISCOURSE—FINAL THOUGHTS

We still need to finish up our examination of this prophecy from Jesus before we can move on to a few other points. I hope you're ready.

"Immediately *after the tribulation* of those days *the sun will be darkened, and the moon will not give its light, and the stars will fall from heaven, and the powers of the heavens will be shaken.* Then will appear in heaven *the sign of the Son of Man,* and then *all the tribes of the earth will mourn,* and they will *see the Son of Man coming on the clouds of heaven with power and great glory.* And he will send out his angels with a loud trumpet call, and *they will gather his elect from the four winds,* from one end of heaven to the other." (Matt. 24:29–31) [emphasis mine]

"But in those days, *after that tribulation, the sun will be darkened, and the moon will not give its light, and the stars will be falling from heaven, and the powers in the heavens will be shaken.* And then they will see *the Son of Man coming in clouds with great power and glory.* And then he will send out the angels and *gather his elect from the four winds,* from the ends of the earth to the ends of heaven." (Mark 13:24–27) [emphasis mine]

"And there will be *signs in sun and moon and stars, and on the earth distress of nations in perplexity because of the roaring of the sea and the waves,* people fainting with fear and with foreboding of what is coming on the world. For the powers of the heavens will be shaken. And then *they will see the Son of Man coming in a cloud with power and great glory.* Now when these things begin to take place, straighten up and raise your heads, because your redemption is drawing near." (Luke 21:25–28) [emphasis mine]

There are a few quick things to mention here. First, that all three Gospels record the fact that, after the tribulation is over—and this is specifically about the persecution of Christians by the Romans and the Jews prior to 70 AD—then we will see things like "the sun will be darkened, and the moon will not give its light and the stars will fall from the sky", and as Luke puts it, "there will be signs in sun, moon and stars."

By now you've probably started to catch on to the fact that whenever we read descriptions of cataclysmic destruction such as this, we're probably venturing into Apocalyptic Hyperbole territory, and you would be right to assume so. This sort of language is used all throughout the Old Testament to describe the destruction of Edom, Babylon, Egypt, and yes, even Jerusalem. In each case, no actual stars fell to the earth, no suns were snuffed out and no moons failed to glow in the night sky.

> BY NOW YOU'VE PROBABLY STARTED TO CATCH ON TO THE FACT THAT WHENEVER WE READ DESCRIPTIONS OF CATACLYSMIC DESTRUCTION SUCH AS THIS, WE'RE PROBABLY VENTURING INTO APOCALYPTIC HYPERBOLE TERRITORY, AND YOU WOULD BE RIGHT TO ASSUME SO.

Once more, hyperbole was used to poetically overstate and emphasize the magnitude of the events taking place by employing very figurative language. It wasn't the end of the world, but what was happening was certainly the end of the world for people living in these places when the armies invaded and the destruction of their cities began.

Here are a few examples if you're curious:

- **In a prophecy against Babylon:** "For the stars of heaven and the constellations thereof shall not give their light: the sun shall be darkened in his going forth, and the moon shall not cause her light to shine. And I will punish the world for their evil, and the wicked for their iniquity; and

I will cause the arrogancy of the proud to cease and will lay low the haughtiness of the terrible." (Isaiah 13:9–11)

- **In a prophecy against Egypt:** "And when I shall put thee [Pharaoh] out, I will cover the heaven, and make the stars thereof dark; I will cover the sun with a cloud, and the moon shall not give her light. All the bright lights of heaven will I make dark over thee, and set darkness upon thy land, saith the LORD God." (Ezekiel 30:18; 32:7–8)

- **In a prophecy against Assyria:** "In that day, declares the Sovereign LORD, I will make the sun go down at noon and darken the earth in broad daylight" (Amos 8:9)

- **In a prophecy against Edom:** "...Hearken, ye people: let the earth hear... All the host of heaven shall be dissolved, and the heavens shall be rolled together as a scroll... For my sword shall be bathed in heaven: behold it shall come down upon Edom, and upon the people of my curse, to judgment... For it is the day of the Lords vengeance." (Isaiah 34:1–8)

- **In a prophecy against Judah:** "I will sweep away everything from the face of the earth, declares the LORD... The wicked will have only heaps of rubble when I cut off man from the face of the earth" (Zephaniah 1:2–3)

- **In another prophecy against Judah:** "The earth shall quake before them; the heavens shall tremble: the sun and the moon shall be dark, and the stars shall withdraw their shining... for the day of the LORD is great and very terrible; and who can abide it?" (Joel 2:4–11)

So, in each of these examples we see repeated, over and over again, references to the sun and the moon going dark and stars falling to the ground and apocalyptic imagery that references the "sweeping away of everything from the face of the earth", and of "the heavens being rolled together like a scroll", but these were localized prophecies about places like Judah, and Edom and Egypt. So, it's highly unlikely that when destruction came to these cities and nations that the entire sky was rolled into a taco or that everything on the face of the earth was swept away, or that the sun and moon failed to shine. At least, not literally. But, in the case of those people who lived in those places when the actual destruction came upon them, it most certainly felt like the end of the world as far as they were concerned.

When Jesus uses this exact same terminology in his Olivet Discourse, the meaning and the intention is the same as in our examples above. This is Apocalyptic Hyperbole, not literal predictions of stars falling out of the sky.

I do want us to keep these verses in mind later when we come to the discussion about what the historian Josephus has to say about the destruction of Jerusalem. Because, even though Jesus does use Apocalyptic Hyperbole here, and there is no need for any literal fulfillment, there were several fascinating events that took place during the siege of Jerusalem according to this non-Christian eye-witness that I think we'll find quite astounding to explore.

As for the rest of this section of the prophecy, we've already talked about what Jesus means when he says that "they will see the Son of Man coming on the clouds of the sky", so there's no need to re-visit that verse.

However, it is worth mentioning the part where he says that "he will send his angels with a loud trumpet call, and they will gather his elect from the four winds…", because this is a reference to the fact that, when this sudden destruction of Jerusalem eventually comes, none of the followers of Jesus ("his elect") will be in harm's way.

This promise was fulfilled when, according to Christian tradition and Church history, the followers of Christ in Jerusalem were warned through several visions and prophecies that the time to flee the city was at hand. This pilgrimage of Christians from Jerusalem to the city of Pella, in the region of the Decapolis, across the Jordan River, is supported by several sources, including these:

> "The people of the Church in Jerusalem were commanded by an oracle given by revelation before the war to those in the city who were worthy of it to depart and dwell in one of the cities of Perea which they called Pella. To it those who believed on Christ traveled from Jerusalem, so that when holy men had altogether deserted the royal capital of the Jews and the whole land of Judaea…" (Eusebius, *Church History 3*, 5, 3)

> "This heresy of the Nazoraeans exists in…the Decapolis in the region of Pella…From there it took its beginning after the exodus from Jerusalem when all the disciples went to live in Pella because Christ had told them to leave Jerusalem and to go away since it would undergo a siege." (Epiphanius, *Panarion 29*, 7–8)

> "For after all those who believed in Christ had generally come to live in Perea, in a city called Pella of the Decapolis of which it is written in the Gospel that it is situated in the neighbourhood of the region of Batanaea and Basanitis, Ebion's preaching originated here after they had moved to this place and had lived there." (Epiphanius, *Panarion 30*, 2-7)

> "So Aquila, while he was in Jerusalem, also saw the disciples of the disciples of the apostles flourishing in the faith and working great signs, healings, and other miracles. For they were such as had come back from the city of Pella to Jerusalem and were living there and teaching. For when the city was about to be taken and destroyed by the Romans, it was revealed in advance

to all the disciples by an angel of God that they should remove from the city, as it was going to be completely destroyed. They sojourned as emigrants in Pella, the city above mentioned in Transjordania. And this city is said to be of the Decapolis." (Epiphanius, *On Weights and Measures,* 15)[12]

THE TRIBES OF THE EARTH

There is also a minor reference in this last section of the Olivet Discourse about how "the tribes of the earth will mourn" (Matt. 24:30) and this is only worth mentioning because Dispensationalists want to say that this verse needs to be a reference to every tribe on earth (literally) in order to be fulfilled. However, the use of the term "tribes of the earth" is a direct reference to the Jewish people.

All throughout Scripture, the term "tribes" always refers to the twelve tribes of Israel, not to the entire world. Only the Israelites are described in this way, and in the context of the destruction of Jerusalem and the Temple, there's no reason to think this is in reference to any other group of people than those who were Jews living in Jerusalem when this event took place.

THIS GENERATION?

The final section of the Olivet Discourse has one final statement that I want to make sure we look at before we move on, and that is where Jesus says:

> "I tell you the truth; this generation will certainly not pass away until all these things have happened. Heaven and earth will pass away, but my words will never pass away." (Matt. 24: 34; Mark 13:30; Luke 21:32)

Some Bible teachers do their very best to squirm out of this statement. Why? Because they really want a generation to stretch out a few thousand years, and they really need all of this to be about something that still hasn't happened yet.

However, if you understand that Jesus is talking only about the coming destruction of Jerusalem and the Temple, and if you understand how to read Apocalyptic Hyperbole correctly, then you've got no problem at all. Because everything Jesus describes in the Olivet Discourse actually *did* transpire within 40 years of his prophecy, so there were some standing there listening to him who were absolutely alive to see every single thing he predicted come to pass in absolute fulfillment of his prediction. This passage is not about the end of the world. It's quite simply a teaching about how the prophecy mentioned in Daniel 9 will be fulfilled in 70 AD when the Romans surround the city of Jerusalem and destroy the Temple, bringing an end to the Jewish age.

Finally, the Olivet Discourse ends with a warning from Jesus that "no one knows the day or the hour" when the destruction of the Temple will take place. Again, this isn't a prediction about when Jesus will return in the sky to rapture us into Heaven. All of this is about 70 AD. Yet, even those who do think Jesus is talking about his Second Coming still can't stop ignoring what Jesus says about the fact that no one can know the day or the hour. They keep trying to set dates and predict when Jesus will come back again. But everything predicted here in the Olivet Discourse has already been fulfilled. There's no reason to look here if we're hoping for any clues about what the return of Jesus will really look like in our own day. That is something I promise we will explore later on in our study. For now, let's dig a little deeper into the events surrounding 70 AD and the invasion of Jerusalem by the Romans.

CHAPTER 6

WHAT ABOUT 70 AD?

"Regrettably, prophetic studies have been so dominated by a naive sensationalism that they have become a source of embarrassment and grief to many in conservative Christendom."

– KEN GENTRY[1]

One of the tragic failures of our New Testament Canon is that it contains several specific prophecies about the details of the coming destruction of Jerusalem and the Temple, and the eventual end of the Jewish age, but all of the historical evidences of the fulfillment of these things are left out completely. Because of this oversight, Dispensationalists are free to speculate about how these prophecies might be fulfilled one day in the future, as all evidence of how it was actually fulfilled is omitted.

To correct this, I'd like to take the next chapter to share some startling historical evidence with you about just how accurately Jesus predicted the events that were soon to take place in Jerusalem, just 40 years after he spoke them to his disciples. Some of the events are brutal and cruel. Others are sensational and difficult to accept. But once you understand what actually transpired during the destruction of Jerusalem in 70 AD, I think you'll agree with me that including this in our New Testament scriptures would have cleared up a lot of confusion regarding End Times prophecy as we know it today.

Thankfully, we have quite an accurate depiction of how these events transpired due to the writings of a Jewish historian named Josephus who was an eyewitness to the entire debacle. He was not sympathetic to Christianity but was a practicing Jew who ended up writing the historical events of his day on behalf of the Romans. So, while his biases might not be in favor of Christianity, his reporting on the events that took place in 70 AD is extremely useful to us. Sometimes it is the very fact that Josephus is *not* a Christian that the things he writes down about the destruction of Jerusalem are most illuminating for us, as you shall see.

Before we get into this too much farther, I do want to take the time to stress that this information isn't something I share gleefully. The destruction of Jerusalem and the Temple was one of the most horrific events in history. What happened to the Jewish people was ugly and brutal. This was not something these people "deserved" nor was it God's punishment, per se, for rejecting Christ and crucifying him on the cross. As we've said previously, God's greatest desire was to help the Jewish people avoid this fate. Jesus saw that this day was coming simply because he understood that they were on a collision course with the Roman Empire and he knew it would end tragically. This is why he sat and wept over the city of Jerusalem on Palm Sunday and said, "If you had known, even you, especially in this your day, the things that make for your peace! But now they are hidden from your eyes." (Luke 19:42)

In the same way that you and I would desperately want to warn those who went to work in the Twin Towers on September 11, 2001 to stay home or to run outside and seek shelter, Jesus came to warn his people that they were headed for a disaster that could be avoided by learning to "think different" (*metanonia* in the Greek) and abandon their desire to violently overthrow the Romans.

To this end, Jesus showed them another way to establish the Kingdom of God on earth: by learning to love their enemies, forgive them, bless them, pray for them and overcome darkness with light. Sadly, because his message was not taken seriously what happened in 70 AD came to pass as he predicted it would. But predicting that your son's hand will burn when he touches the stove is not the same thing as making him touch it, or causing the burn to appear on his hand.

This is simple cause and effect. We lament that things turned out this way, but we do need to at least admit that Jesus accurately predicted how and when it would happen.

> TO THIS END, JESUS SHOWED THEM ANOTHER WAY TO ESTABLISH THE KINGDOM OF GOD ON EARTH: BY LEARNING TO LOVE THEIR ENEMIES, FORGIVE THEM, BLESS THEM, PRAY FOR THEM AND OVERCOME DARKNESS WITH LIGHT.

To begin, let's start with a little history about how the city of Jerusalem came to be surrounded by the Romans in the first place.

In the year 66 AD the Jews of Judea launched a massive rebellion against their Roman oppressors. In response, the Emperor Nero dispatched an army under the generalship of Vespasian to restore order.

By the year 68 AD, resistance in the northern part of the province had been eradicated and the Romans turned their full attention to the subjugation of Jerusalem. That same year, the Emperor Nero died by his own hand, creating a power vacuum in Rome.

In the resulting chaos, Vespasian was declared Emperor and returned to the Imperial City. This meant that it was his son,

Titus, who was called upon to lead the remaining army in the assault on Jerusalem.

Under the command of Titus, the Roman legions surrounded the city of Jerusalem and began to slowly squeeze the life out of the Jewish stronghold. By the year 70 AD, the attackers had breached Jerusalem's outer walls and began a systematic ransacking of the city. This assault culminated in the burning and destruction of the Temple that served as the center of Judaism.

In victory, the Romans slaughtered thousands. Of those spared from death: thousands more were enslaved and sent to toil in the mines of Egypt, others were dispersed to arenas throughout the Empire to be butchered for the amusement of the public. The Temple's sacred relics were taken to Rome where they were displayed in celebration of the victory.

The Jewish rebellion sputtered on for another three years and was finally extinguished in 73 AD with the fall of the various pockets of resistance including the stronghold at Masada.

As we've said, our only first-hand account of the Roman assault on the Temple comes from the Jewish historian Josephus Flavius; a former leader of the Jewish Revolt who had surrendered to the Romans and had won favor from Emperor Vespasian. In gratitude, Josephus took Vespasian's family name—Flavius—as his own.

We join the account of Josephus as the Romans fight their way into the inner sanctum of the Temple:

> "...the rebels shortly after attacked the Romans again, and a clash followed between the guards of the sanctuary and the troops who were putting out the fire inside the inner court; the latter routed the Jews and followed in hot pursuit right up to the Temple itself. Then one of the soldiers, without awaiting any orders and with no dread of so momentous a deed, but urged on by some supernatural force, snatched a blazing piece of wood and, climbing on another soldier's back, hurled the

flaming brand through a low golden window that gave access, on the north side, to the rooms that surrounded the sanctuary.

"As the flames shot up, the Jews let out a shout of dismay that matched the tragedy; they flocked to the rescue, with no thought of sparing their lives or husbanding their strength; for the sacred structure that they had constantly guarded with such devotion was vanishing before their very eyes.

"...No exhortation or threat could now restrain the impetuosity of the legions; for passion was in supreme command. Crowded together around the entrances, many were trampled down by their companions; others, stumbling on the smoldering and smoked-filled ruins of the porticoes, died as miserably as the defeated. As they drew closer to the Temple, they pretended not even to hear Caesar's orders, but urged the men in front to throw in more firebrands.

"The rebels were powerless to help; carnage and flight spread throughout. Most of the slain were peaceful citizens, weak and unarmed, and they were butchered where they were caught. The heap of corpses mounted higher and higher about the altar; a stream of blood flowed down the Temple's steps, and the bodies of those slain at the top slipped to the bottom.

"When Caesar failed to restrain the fury of his frenzied soldiers, and the fire could not be checked, he entered the building with his generals and looked at the holy place of the sanctuary and all its furnishings, which exceeded by far the accounts current in foreign lands and fully justified their splendid repute in our own.

"As the flames had not yet penetrated to the inner sanctum, but were consuming the chambers that surrounded the sanctuary, Titus assumed correctly that there was still time to save the structure; he ran out and by personal appeals he endeavored to persuade his men to put out the fire, instructing Liberalius, a centurion of his bodyguard of lancers, to club any of the men who disobeyed his orders. But their respect for Caesar and their fear of the centurion's staff who was trying to check them were overpowered by their rage, their detestation of the Jews, and an utterly uncontrolled lust for battle.

"Most of them were spurred on, moreover, by the expectation of loot, convinced that the interior was full of money and dazzled by observing that everything around them was made of gold. But they were forestalled by one of those who had entered into the building, and who, when Caesar dashed out to restrain the troops, pushed a firebrand, in the darkness, into the hinges of the gate Then, when the flames suddenly shot up from the interior, Caesar and his generals withdrew, and no one was left to prevent those outside from kindling the blaze. Thus, in defiance of Caesar's wishes, the Temple was set on fire.

"While the Temple was ablaze, the attackers plundered it, and countless people who were caught by them were slaughtered. There was no pity for age and no regard was accorded rank; children and old men, laymen and priests, alike were butchered; every class was pursued and crushed in the grip of war, whether they cried out for mercy or offered resistance.

"Through the roar of the flames streaming far and wide, the groans of the falling victims were heard; such was the height of the hill and the magnitude of the blazing pile that the entire city seemed to be ablaze; and the noise—nothing more deafening and frightening could be imagined.

"There were the war cries of the Roman legions as they swept onwards en masse, the yells of the rebels encircled by fire and sword, the panic of the people who, cut off above, fled into the arms of the enemy, and their shrieks as they met their fate. The cries on the hill blended with those of the multitudes in the city below; and now many people who were exhausted and tongue-tied as a result of hunger, when they beheld the Temple on fire, found strength once more to lament and wail. Peraea and the surrounding hills, added their echoes to the deafening din. But more horrifying than the din were the sufferings.

"The Temple Mount, everywhere enveloped in flames, seemed to be boiling over from its base; yet the blood seemed more abundant than the flames and the numbers of the slain greater than those of the slayers. The soldiers climbed over heaps of bodies as they chased the fugitives."[2]

It's worth mentioning that when this battle was over, Titus refused to accept a wreath of victory for his role in the destruction of Jerusalem saying that his victory did not come through his own efforts but that he had merely "served as an instrument of God's wrath."[3]

What's even more stunning is the fact that the day the Temple in Jerusalem was destroyed was the exact same day and month as when the previous Temple was destroyed by the Babylonians. That day is known as "Tisa B'Av"[4] or "The Ninth of Av" to the Jewish people and there is a fast that is observed to commemorate the destruction of both the First and the Second Temples[5] which occurred on the 9th of the Jewish month of Av[6], exactly 655 years apart.

Honestly, when I first learned that the date of the destruction of the First Temple was exactly the same as the date of the destruction of the Second Temple, I could hardly believe it. This could not merely be a coincidence. It spoke to the intentionality and specificity of the prophetic events coinciding and overlapping together in an astounding way that I could not, and cannot, reconcile in any other way than to admit that these events were foretold and ordained and fulfilled in miraculous fashion.

But, there are a few other specific details mentioned by Josephus about the destruction of the Temple that I believe you'll find equally astounding.

THE SEVEN SIGNS OF JOSEPHUS

Josephus prefaces these seven signs by saying in his book *The Jewish War*:

"Thus it was that the wretched people were deluded at that time by charlatans and pretended messengers [false prophets] of the deity; while they neither heeded nor believed in the manifest portents that foretold the coming desolation, but, as if thunderstruck and bereft of eyes and mind, disregarded the plain warnings of God."[7]

What's fascinating is that Josephus confirms that Jesus was indeed correct when he predicted that "many false prophets would come" and "deceive even the elect if that were possible" in the Olivet Discourse. He also affirms that the people appeared to be virtually blind to these signs that, he says, were sent to them from God to warn them of the coming destruction of their city and their Temple.

Here are the *Seven Signs* that Josephus records as happening in Jerusalem in the years and months leading up to the day that the Temple was destroyed. They are astounding and perplexing, but many of them appear to overlap with things that Jesus said would come to pass.

Let's take a look:

1) A SWORD IN THE SKY

"So it was when a star resembling a sword, stood over the city [Jerusalem] and a comet which continued for a year."[8] [In 66 AD]

What I find fascinating about this sign is that a sword, if you hold it vertically, tends to have the same shape as a cross does. If swords and crosses are similarly shaped, then perhaps this statement by Jesus in the Olivet Discourse was also intended to be a reference to this sign of the sword in the sky:

> "Then will appear *the sign of the Son of Man in heaven*. And then all the peoples of the earth will mourn when they see the Son of Man coming on the clouds of heaven, with power and great glory." (Matt. 24:30) [emphasis mine]

As we've already seen, the idea of the "Son of Man coming on the clouds of heaven" is a reference to the judgment of Jerusalem which was physically manifested in the Roman Army which surrounded the city and destroyed it. But this additional detail about the image of a sword appearing above the city prior to the destruction of Jerusalem is quite startling, isn't it? I think so. We also see that Josephus mentions a comet that continued to remain visible over the sky in Jerusalem for a year. This fulfills the prediction that there would be signs in the heavens prior to the destruction of the Temple. Anyway, here's the second sign:

2) A BRIGHT LIGHT

> "So again when, before the revolt and the commotion that led to war [i.e., before the war], at the time when the people were assembling for the feast of unleavened bread, on the eighth of the month Xanthieus [Nisan], at the ninth hour of the night [3 AM]… so brilliant a light shown round the [holy] altar and the sanctuary[of the temple] that it seemed to be broad daylight; and this continued for half an hour. By the inexperienced, this was regarded as a good omen, but by the sacred scribes it was at once interpreted in accordance with after[later] events."[9]

As far as I can tell, this bright light that shines in darkness isn't something specifically predicted by anything Jesus said in the Olivet Discourse. However, it could be a very slight nod to a verse in Isaiah which says "those in darkness have seen a great light," (Isa. 9:2), and the Gospel of John which affirmed that in Christ a great "light shines in the darkness, but the darkness has not understood it." (John 1:5, NKJV) Or, it could be another reference to signs in the heavens that preceded the destruction of Jerusalem.

3) A COW GIVES BIRTH TO A LAMB

> "At that same feast [just after the 2nd sign, the great light over the altar] a cow that had been brought by someone for sacrifice gave birth [just before it was to be killed] to a lamb in the midst in the court of the Temple."[10]

This sign is almost too fantastic to believe. But, Josephus believes it did indeed happen and he was an eye-witness to the events leading up to and during the actual destruction of Jerusalem, so take it as you like. However, this sign does appear to have been something that people reported as having happened just after the great light spoken about above.

We can only speculate as to why God might give such a sign to his people, except perhaps to exhaust every possible avenue for alerting them about the coming destruction. There's much symbolism in this sign that we could unpack, but whatever it meant, the people in Jerusalem at this time missed its meaning entirely.

4) THE EASTERN GATE OPENS BY ITSELF

> "The eastern gate of the inner court—it was of brass and very massive, and, when closed towards evening, could scarcely be moved by 20 men; fastened with iron-bound bars [on each side], it had bolts which were sunk to a great depth into a threshold consisting of a solid block of stone—this gate was observed at the sixth hour of the night [midnight] to have opened of its own accord. The watchmen of the temple ran and reported the

matter to the captain, and he came up and with difficulty succeeded in shutting it."

"This again to the uninitiated seemed the best of omens, as they supposed that God had opened to them the gate of blessings." "But the learned understood that the security of the Temple was dissolving of its own accord and that the opening of the gate meant a present to the enemy, interpreting the portent [sign, the same word as in the gospel] in their own minds as indicative of coming desolation."[11]

Josephus seems quite frustrated that this particular sign was not only ignored by his people, but that somehow they had found a way to convince themselves it was a good omen rather than a bad one.

5) ARMIES IN THE SKY

"Again, not many days after that festival on the twenty-first of Artemisium [the Jewish month of Iyyar which is in the late springtime], there appeared a miraculous phenomenon, passing belief. Indeed, what I am about to relate would, I imagine, have been deemed a fable, were it not for the narratives of eyewitnesses and for the subsequent calamities which deserved to be so signalized... For before sunset throughout all parts of the country [of Judea] chariots were seen in the air and armed battalions hurtling through the clouds and encompassing the cities."[12]

Even Josephus freely admits that he has a hard time believing such a sign, but nevertheless reports it as having taken place. This was a vision in the sky, over the city, which included sight and sound in an unprecedented fashion. It's difficult to know how people at the time processed these increasingly ominous series of supernatural events leading up to the destruction of the city. We do know, because Josephus tells us, that many of the Jewish people did flee the city out of fear, both just before and even during the long siege of Jerusalem by the Romans. Still, roughly 1.1 million people were slaughtered on that fateful day, so only a handful made their escape before the final onslaught.

6) VOICES SPEAKING

"Moreover, at the feast which is called Pentecost the priests [all 24 of them] on entering the inner court of the Temple by night as their custom was in the discharge of their ministrations, reported that they were conscious, first of a commotion and a din [a great noise], and after that of a voice as of a host [an army], 'We are departing hence [from here]."[13]

It is interesting that this sign took place on the day of Pentecost exactly 33 years from the time the Spirit was poured out on all flesh in Jerusalem and this sign occurred.

Also fascinating is that the sign at Pentecost in the book of Acts was the sound of many languages being released upon the Disciples as they spoke in many different tongues, and here the sign is once more of voices in the air, but this time all speaking audibly and in their own language a warning to leave this place at once. A warning which, sadly, was not heeded by most people at this time.

7) THE LAST PROPHET: JESUS/JOSHUA

This last sign is a doozy. It's one that starts four years before the start of the final destruction and continues daily, right up until the actual day the "Abomination of Desolation" takes place. Keep in mind, that the name "Joshua" in the Hebrew is an alternate form of the name "Jesus."

"But a further portent was even more alarming. Four years before the war [in Tabernacles time in 62 CE] when the city was enjoying profound peace and prosperity, there came to the feast at which it was the custom of all Jews to erect tabernacles to God, one Joshua, [Another way of saying 'Jesus' or 'Y'Shua'] son of Ananias, a rude peasant, who, standing in the Temple, suddenly began to cry out, 'A voice from the east, a voice from the west, a voice from the four winds; a voice against Jerusalem and the sanctuary, a voice against the bridegroom and the bride, a voice against all the people.'

"Day and night he went about all the alleys with this cry on his lips. Some of the leading citizens, incensed at these ill-omened words, arrested the fellow and severely chastised him. But he without a word on his own behalf or for the private ear of those who smote him only continued his cries as before.

"Thereupon, the magistrates, supposing, as was indeed the case that the man was under some supernatural impulse, brought him before the Roman governor; there, although flayed to the bone with scourges, he neither sued for mercy nor shed a tear, but, merely introducing the most mournful of variations into his ejaculation [words from his mouth], responded to each stroke with 'Woe to Jerusalem!'

"When Albinus, the [Roman] governor asked him who [he was] and whence he was [where he came from] and why he uttered these cries, he answered him never a word, but unceasingly reiterated his dirge over the city, until Albinus pronounced him a maniac and let him go.

"During the whole period up to the outbreak of the war he neither approached nor was seen talking to any of the citizens, but daily, like a prayer... repeated his lament, 'Woe to Jerusalem!' He neither cursed any of those who beat him from day to day, nor blessed those who offered him food: to all men that melancholy presage was his one reply. His cries were loudest at the festivals.

"So for seven years and five months he continued his wail, his voice never flagging nor his strength exhausted, until the siege, having seen his presage verified, he found his rest. For, while going his round and shouting in piercing tones from the wall, 'Woe once more to the city and to the people and to the Temple,' as he added a last word, 'and woe to me also,' a stone hurled from the ballista struck and killed him on the spot. So with those ominous words still on his lips he passed away." [14]

How fascinating! One final "Jesus" is sent to the people to pronounce daily, unending "woe" upon them right up until the armies are actually surrounding the city.

If nothing else, we have here a literal "second coming of Jesus" prior to the destruction of the Temple, even if in name only.

These *Seven Signs* of Josephus shed new light on the events that transpired in Jerusalem right up until the fulfillment of Jesus's prophecy in the Olivet Discourse. Much of it confirms details mentioned by Jesus and some of it adds even more mystery to the event.

But the one thing we can see here is that God went out of His way to warn the Jewish people, first through Daniel, then through Jesus, then through the ministry of the Apostles, and then finally through these *Seven Signs* recorded here. Clearly God did everything He could possibly do to warn His people to turn back and reconsider their actions. God did *not* want this to happen and yet in spite of everything God did to try to stop it, the people refused to give up on their violent desires to overthrow their Roman oppressors. If they had known the things that make for peace, as Jesus lamented, there is not a doubt in my mind that things could have turned out very differently. Unfortunately, we'll never know.

> IF NOTHING ELSE, WE HAVE HERE A LITERAL "SECOND COMING OF JESUS" PRIOR TO THE DESTRUCTION OF THE TEMPLE, EVEN IF IN NAME ONLY.

CONFIRMATION FROM TACITUS

The Roman historian Tacitus also confirms that there were many signs given to the Jewish people prior to the tragic events of 70 AD.

> "There were many prodigies presignifying their ruin which was not averted by all the sacrifices and vows of that people. Armies were seen fighting in the air with brandished weapons. A fire fell upon the Temple from the clouds. The doors of the Temple were suddenly opened. At the same time there was a loud voice saying that the gods were removing, which was accompanied with a sound as of a multitude going out. All which things were supposed, by some to portend great calamities." [15]

I find it fascinating that both Josephus—a non-Christian Jewish historian—and Tacitus himself would record these signs that preceded the ultimate destruction of Jerusalem and the end of the Jewish Age. But what I find even more flabbergasting is that none of this is ever communicated to the average Christian in our Church today. Instead of historical records like these that shed more light on the statements Jesus made in the Olivet Discourse, we're fed a steady diet of End Times hype and nonsense. This is how Christians today are totally unaware of the fact that the day the Temple was destroyed in 70 AD was the exact same day and month that the previous Jewish Temple was destroyed. How can this be? Why would we ignore this?

Well, I would argue that all of this is because our seminaries and pulpits favor a certain narrative that leans towards Darby's Dispensational Futurism, and because of this all other information—no matter how enriching it might be to our faith—is selectively edited out and replaced with sermons about Blood Moons and how what's happening in the Middle East is proof that the Second Coming of Jesus is closer than ever.

Hopefully books like this one will help to expose this practice and illuminate our minds regarding what the Olivet Discourse is really all about and how everything Jesus said was going to happen has already happened, just as he predicted it would.

If we're willing to ignore evidence that exalts Jesus as a prophet whose testimony is validated by historical events simply because it interferes with our particular End Times narrative, then perhaps we need to take a step back and reevaluate our priorities.

So, let's see what we've learned so far: The Seventy Weeks of Daniel prophecy was about the timing of Messiah's appearance. This was counted between the time the Emperor (whether Artexerxes or Cyrus) gave the decree to rebuild the city of Jerusalem and the appearance of Jesus 490 years later. Everything prophesied by Daniel in his Seventy Weeks vision was fulfilled by Jesus, including the cessation of the daily sacrifice in the Temple, the establishing of a covenant (the New Covenant proclaimed by Jesus in the upper room), being "cut off" after three and a half years (because Jesus's ministry only lasted that long and was cut short when he was crucified), and the events that would eventually lead to the "Abomination of Desolation" were "set up" because of how the Jewish people responded to his message, (which was sadly a rejection of him and his call to love their enemies).

> IF WE'RE WILLING TO IGNORE EVIDENCE THAT EXALTS JESUS AS A PROPHET WHOSE TESTIMONY IS VALIDATED BY HISTORICAL EVENTS SIMPLY BECAUSE IT INTERFERES WITH OUR PARTICULAR END TIMES NARRATIVE, THEN PERHAPS WE NEED TO TAKE A STEP BACK AND REEVALUATE OUR PRIORITIES.

We also learned that the Olivet Discourse spoken by Jesus (and recorded in Matthew, Mark and Luke) was about the coming destruction of the Temple by the Romans, and the specific signs and details about events leading up to that day. Jesus predicted the signs, the timeline and the sequence of events accurately, as evidenced by what we see recorded in history.

One of those historians, Josephus, provides even more fascinating detail about the events of the destruction of Jerusalem and the Temple and adds an additional Seven Signs given by God to warn the Jewish people to turn back from their lust for revolution and how, sadly, they did not heed these warnings.

Now that we've completed our look at the Olivet Discourse and the Seventy Weeks of Daniel prophecies, let's turn our attention to a few other questions, like "What is the Mark of the Beast?", "Who is the Anti-Christ?", "What is the Day of the Lord?" and how should we read and understand prophetic books like Revelation? All this and a lot more will be covered in our next few chapters.

CHAPTER 7

THE MARK OF THE BEAST, THE ANTI-CHRIST, AND THE DAY OF THE LORD

"The literature of the Apocalypse, especially in English, is immense, but mostly impository rather than expository, and hence worthless or even mischievous, [and] confounding and misleading."

– PHILIP SCHAFF[1]

Because so many of us have grown up in the Evangelical Christian Church, these narratives of End Times events are indelibly seared into our brains from an early age. We're told that certain things need to happen before Jesus can return for us and Rapture us into the sky. We're assured that these things are bound to happen very soon and that one day in the near future we'll see the rise of the Anti-Christ, the Tribulation will begin, the Mark of the Beast will start to be imposed upon us, and those who take this mark will be cursed for all eternity.

Of course, most of this is going to take place whenever this mysterious Anti-Christ figure sets up the Temple in Jerusalem, makes a peace treaty with Israel, establishes a one world government, and then suddenly breaks his treaty and sets himself up as

God by performing some "abomination that causes desolation" in the newly-rebuilt Temple.

Now, as we've already seen, most of that story comes from misunderstanding and misapplying prophecies found in the Seventy Weeks of Daniel and the Olivet Discourse. So, hopefully, we're not worried that any of these things are still going to take place. However, there are some elements of this End Times Dispensational narrative that we haven't yet examined in detail. That's what we're going to do in this chapter.

> OF COURSE, THESE NARRATIVES MAY BE DIFFICULT TO SHAKE FOR SOME OF US. EVEN WHEN WE CAN SEE THAT THE VERSES AREN'T ACTUALLY SAYING WHAT WE'VE BEEN TOLD THEY ARE SAYING, IT CAN STILL BE HARD TO LET GO OF THEM.

Of course, these narratives may be difficult to shake for some of us. Even when we can see that the verses aren't actually saying what we've been told they are saying, it can still be hard to let go of them. We'll talk about why this is and how we can overcome it in an upcoming chapter. But, for now, let's do our best to relax our grip on those versions of the End Times story we've heard and embraced for so long and try to take an objective look at what the scriptures are really trying to say to us.

Ready? Ok, here we go.

THE MARK OF THE BEAST

When John wrote the epistle of Revelation to the seven churches, he made it very clear—on numerous occasions—that the prophecies contained in his letter were to take place "soon". For example: In verse 1, John says:

> "The Revelation of Jesus Christ, which God gave Him to show to His bond-servants, the things *which must shortly take place...*"

In verse 3 he says:

"...and heed the things which are written in it; for *the time is near.*" [emphasis mine]

John uses specific words in the Greek throughout his epistle which mean: "shortly", "without delay", "soon", "in a short time", "near", "about to", etc.

There can be little doubt, therefore, that the First Century Christians who received and read John's letter understood at least one thing: They were reading about events that were about to happen very, very soon.

Keeping this in mind, let's see if we can identify "The Beast" from Revelation. First, since John is writing about events that were about to happen quickly, we can be reasonably sure that "The Beast" was a contemporary of John. Secondly, John describes this as either a person (Rev. 13:18), or as several people (Rev. 17:10), or as a government or kingdom (Rev. 17:9).

Christians in the First Century would have been very familiar with Old Testament references in Daniel to the Four Beasts (Dan. 7:17) which corresponded to the Four Kingdoms or Empires. Therefore, those readers would have known that John's references to "The Beast" in his letters pointed to the Empire of their own day—The Roman Empire.

But what about the person who is referred to as "The Beast"? Well, since the John was writing this letter from captivity on the Island of Patmos, he reverted to code which his readers (Jewish Christians) would understand easily but his captors (the Romans) would not.

Note also that, as a prisoner of Rome, John wouldn't want to come right out and write anything negative about the Emperor or the government that held him captive—for obvious reasons.

This is why, when he wants to let Christians know that "The Beast" is the Emperor Nero, he would say:

> "Here is wisdom. Let him who has understanding calculate the number of the beast, for the number is that of a man; and his number is six hundred and sixty-six." (Rev. 13:18)

The Hebrew spelling of "Nero Caesar" was NRWN QSR. Since Hebrew letters doubled as numbers it was a simple thing to take that name and add them together which adds up exactly to 666. (Example: N = 50, R = 200, W = 6, N =50, Q = 100, S = 60, R = 200)

One fascinating variant of this same passage notes that, "Some manuscripts read: 616" rather than 666. Why is this? Because when Revelation was later copied into Latin the name Nero Caesar didn't add up to 666, it added up to 616. So, to make it easier for those later Latin-speaking (non-Hebrew reading) Christians to arrive at the same conclusion the number was changed to 616 in certain translations.

Want more proof? Ok. In Revelation 17:9–10 John tells us:

> "Here is the mind which has wisdom. The seven heads are seven mountains, on which the woman sits, and they are seven kings; five have fallen, one is, the other has not yet come; and when he comes, he must remain a little while."

You've probably heard that the "seven mountains" correspond to the Seven Hills of Rome. However, did you know that the seven kings also point to Nero as "The Beast"? They do. Because John tells us in the verse above that: "Five have fallen, one is, the other has not yet come and when he comes, he must remain a little while." Why is this important? Because according to Josephus, the Roman historian, Julius Caesar was the first king, followed by Augustus, Tiberius, Caligula and Claudius. The sixth king? That was Nero. So, that means that he is the "one [who] is" referred to in the passage above.

The seventh king—the one who followed Nero—was Galba, and as John prophesied, he reigned for a short time (about seven months). Nero, as the sixth king of Rome, was the first to persecute Christians in the First Century. He started persecuting them in November of 64 AD and ended on June 8, 68 AD when he killed himself. That was *42 months* of persecution. Notice what John says about "The Beast":

> "And there was given to him a mouth speaking arrogant words and blasphemies; and authority to act for *forty-two months* was given him." (Rev. 13:5)

Coincidence? I think not. Clearly John is going out of his way to let his readers know that "The Beast" had a name that, in the Hebrew, added up to a number (666) and that he was the sixth, and current king of Rome, and that his persecution would last exactly 42 months. What could be clearer than this?

EXTRA-BIBLICAL PROOF

If we need a little more convincing, please consider that Nero was also called "The Beast" by contemporary pagan writer Apollonius of Tyana, who said of Nero:

> "In my travels… I have seen many wild beasts of Arabia and India; but this beast, that is commonly called a Tyrant, I know not how many heads it has, nor if it be crooked of claw, and armed with horrible fangs… And of wild beasts you cannot say that they were ever known to eat their own mother, but Nero gorged himself on this diet." [2]

Note that Nero murdered his own parents, and his brother, and his pregnant wife, in addition to several other family members. We also have evidence from the Romans that Nero enjoyed dressing up as a wild beast and raping male and female prisoners.

Still not convinced? Consider that all of the earliest Church Fathers from Irenaeus in the First Century, all the way through to St. Beatus in the 8th century agreed that "The Beast" was Nero.

BUYING AND SELLING?

Roman citizens were required to publicly claim allegiance to Caesar by burning incense in his honor and proclaiming that "Caesar is Lord". Those who did this received a document that allowed them to buy and sell in the marketplace. Without it, no one could purchase anything. Therefore, the "Mark of the Beast"—or the document that showed your allegiance to Nero as Lord—was required to buy and sell if you lived during the time when John wrote his epistle to the seven churches.

> SO, LET'S BE VERY CLEAR. THE MARK OF THE BEAST IS NOT A MICROCHIP. IT IS NOT A BARCODE. IT IS NOT YOUR CREDIT CARD. THE BEAST WAS EMPEROR NERO.

None of those Christians who read Revelation were confused about what John meant by this. It was already happening to them.

WHAT THIS MEANS

So, let's be very clear. The Mark of the Beast is not a microchip. It is not a barcode. It is not your credit card. The Beast was Emperor Nero. The Mark of the Beast was "the number of his name" which added up to 666. We're told that The Beast would reign in terror for 42 months and Nero's persecution of the Church lasted exactly 42 months. Please do not fall for those online posts that try to scare you into believing that the Mark of the Beast is coming to your town, or that we're in the End Times because some new technology makes it easy for people to do their banking with a chip or a scanner. This is not a sign of the Second Coming. It has nothing to do with anything we read about in the book of Revelation. It's simply the advance of technology that exists to make our lives easier. Perhaps the only thing sinister about any of this is the possibility that someone will get filthy rich promoting these technologies, but it won't lead to the rise of an Anti-Christ figure or the loss of your salvation if you start using it.

Speaking of the Anti-Christ, who is it? What does the Scripture actually tell us about him? That's the question we're going to answer next.

WHO IS THE ANTI-CHRIST?

One of the main characters in Darby's Dispensational version of the End Times is none other than the mysterious "Anti-Christ" figure who will show up one day to deceive the nations, establish himself as God, and usher in the inevitable return of Jesus to the Earth. But, is this something the Bible actually teaches? Actually, no, it doesn't.

The word "Anti-Christ" only appears in two books of the New Testament, and neither are the ones you'd expect to find them in. Only 1 John and 2 John make any reference to the "Anti-Christ" so before we go any further let's look at what they have to say:

"Little children, it is the last hour; and as you have heard that the Antichrist is coming, even now many antichrists have come, by which we know that it is the last hour." (1 John 2:18)

Ok, wait a second. John says that "it *is* the last hour" already and that "many antichrists have come" and in fact that it's because of this fact that "we know that it is the last hour." How can this be? Perhaps the "last hour" when "many antichrists" come was something that happened in our past, but in his future?

Hmm... let's keep reading, there's more:

"Who is a liar but he who denies that Jesus is the Christ? He is antichrist who denies the Father and the Son." (1 John 2:22)

Ok, we're getting a little more detail now about how to identify the "Anti-Christ." John says that it's anyone who denies that Jesus is the Messiah (or the Christ). Now, for the record, at the time that this was written, there were several people who denied that Jesus was the Messiah, and those people were the unbelieving Jews who also persecuted the early Christians as we read in the book of Acts. In other words, it has nothing to do with any End Times figure of the Apocalypse who is about to rise up and signal the Second Coming of Christ. This is a very generic term for anyone—male or female, young or old—who denies that Jesus was the Messiah.

Let's look at the very last reference from 1 John about the Anti-Christ:

"...and every spirit that does not confess that Jesus Christ has come in the flesh is not of God. And this is the spirit of the Antichrist, which you have heard was coming, and is now already in the world." (1 John 4:3)

SO, ONCE MORE, THE IDENTITY OF THE ANTI-CHRIST IS NOT A SINGLE PERSON WHO WILL ARISE AT THE END OF TIME TO USHER IN THE SECOND COMING OF JESUS. NOT AT ALL.

So, once more, the identity of the Anti-Christ is not a single person who will arise at the end of time to usher in the Second Coming of Jesus. Not at all. In fact, no mention is made about any of those things in either of these passages. What we read about is how those who deny that Jesus was the Christ are Anti-Christ, and anyone who does not agree that Jesus has come in the flesh is Anti-Christ and—most importantly—that the "last hour" was back when this epistle was written and the evidence of that was the fact that "many antichrists" were already present at that time.

Let me suggest that what John is writing about here is exactly what Jesus was talking about in his Olivet Discourse—the destruction of the Temple and the end of the age (not the end of the world). It is the "last hour" for John because he can see that everything is starting to take shape just as Jesus had predicted it would when he told his Disciples about the signs of the end which would be marked by the events of 70 AD.

Now, there is one final reference to the Anti-Christ that we need to look at which is found in 2 John. Here it is:

> "For many deceivers have gone out into the world who do not confess Jesus Christ as coming in the flesh. This is a deceiver and an antichrist." (2 John 7)

That's it. There are no other references in the entire Bible about the Anti-Christ. So, once again, we need to take a step back and realize that the version of the End Times we inherited from John Nelson Darby isn't based on anything the Bible actually tells us. It's a constructed narrative where one thing is taken from this passage and another is lifted from yet another verse and everything is thrown into a large soup bowl of eschatology that bears little resemblance to what the original authors wanted to say.

Now, we do need to take a look at an Old Testament event called "The Day of the Lord". We need to ask ourselves how this ties into the events of 70 AD versus what Dispensationalism teaches.

THE DAY OF THE LORD

There are a total of 35 references in the Scriptures to something described as "The Day of the Lord" and if we were to examine those in detail there a few things we might start to notice. For example, all of these references to the "Day of the Lord" describe a day of wailing, weeping, destruction and fierce judgment. None of these describe anything even remotely as joyful or exciting as the Second Coming of Christ who comes in the clouds to Rapture all the Christians into Heaven at the sound of the trumpet or the shout of the Archangel. Instead, we read things like this:

> "For the *day of the LORD* of hosts Shall come upon everything proud and lofty, Upon everything lifted up—And it shall be brought low." (Isaiah 2:12) [emphasis mine]

> "Wail, for the *day of the LORD* is at hand! It will come as destruction from the Almighty." (Isaiah 13:6) [emphasis mine]

> "Behold, the *day of the LORD* comes, Cruel, with both wrath and fierce anger, To lay the land desolate; And He will destroy its sinners from it." (Isaiah 13:9) [emphasis mine]

> "For it is the *day of the LORD's* vengeance, The year of recompense for the cause of Zion." (Isaiah 34:8) [emphasis mine]

> "For this is the *day of the LORD* God of hosts, A day of vengeance, That He may avenge Himself on His adversaries. The sword shall devour; It shall be satiated and made drunk with their blood." (Jeremiah 46:10) [emphasis mine]

> "Alas for the day! For the *day of the LORD* is at hand; It shall come as destruction from the Almighty." (Joel 1:15) [emphasis mine]

> "Blow the trumpet in Zion, And sound an alarm in My holy mountain! Let all the inhabitants of the land tremble; For the *day of the LORD* is coming…" (Joel 2:1) [emphasis mine]

> "The LORD gives voice before His army, For His camp is very great; For strong is the One who executes His word. For the *day of the LORD* is great and very terrible; Who can endure it?" (Joel 2:11) [emphasis mine]

"The sun shall be turned into darkness, And the moon into blood, Before the coming of the great and awesome *day of the* LORD." (Joel 2:31) [emphasis mine]

"Woe to you who desire the *day of the* LORD! For what good is the *day of the* LORD to you? It will be darkness, and not light." (Amos 5:18) [emphasis mine]

Now, this is just a sampling of verses from the Old Testament concerning the "Day of the Lord" and if we're paying attention we'll notice just how much it sounds like what Jesus was talking about in the Olivet Discourse. Some of these passages even use the phrases about the signs in the sun and the moon, which Jesus makes reference to as well. Another thing we should notice is that some of these passages specifically are about a "Day of the Lord" where the judgment was against Babylon or Egypt or some other city in some other time in history. So, the phrase in general appears to be a reference to any day where great destruction comes upon a city or a nation. However, several of these verses above are specifically applied to the events of 70 AD by the Disciples and by the Apostle Paul, which we will examine in greater detail below.

First, let's look at this reference from Malachi which is directly tied to the coming of John the Baptist who "prepared the way" for Jesus.

"Behold, I will send you Elijah the prophet Before the coming of the great and dreadful *day of the* LORD." (Malachi 4:5) [emphasis mine]

You may remember that all through the ministry of Jesus there is always the question as to whether or not Elijah had come to signal the coming of the Messiah as prophesied in this verse above. Jesus makes it plain that John the Baptist *was* the fulfillment of this promise to send one like Elijah prior to the "great and dreadful day of the Lord"—a reference to the impending destruction of Jerusalem which Jesus predicted in his Olivet Discourse.

> "And if you are willing to receive it, he [John the Baptist] is Elijah who is to come." (Matthew 11:14)

> "But I say to you that Elijah has come already, and they did not know him but did to him whatever they wished. Likewise the Son of Man is also about to suffer at their hands." (Matthew 17:12)

Of course, we also see that Elijah himself did appear alongside Moses during the Transfiguration of Jesus on the Mount as recorded in Matthew 17:3. So, Elijah did come, as promised in Malachi 4:5 before the great and dreadful day of the Lord—first in the form of John the Baptist, as Jesus confirms, and also in the Transfiguration account found in Matthew chapter 11.

Here's another interesting reference to look at:

> "For the day is near, Even the *day of the* LORD is near; It will be a day of clouds, the time of the Gentiles." (Ezekiel 30:3) [emphasis mine]

Notice in this passage that the "Day of the Lord" is described as "a time of the Gentiles", which was also referenced by Jesus in his Olivet Discourse when he referred to "the trampling of Jerusalem until the times of the Gentiles shall be fulfilled." (See Luke 21:24) Clearly this ties the Day of the Lord to the eventual destruction of Jerusalem by the Gentiles in 70 AD.

One of the most important references to the Day of the Lord we need to examine is found in the New Testament when the Apostle Peter references Joel chapter 2 in reference to what people are experiencing during the Day of Pentecost:

> "But Peter, standing up with the eleven, raised his voice and said to them, "Men of Judea and all who dwell in Jerusalem, let this be known to you, and heed my words. For these are not drunk, as you suppose, since it is only the third hour of the day. *But*

this is what was spoken by the prophet Joel: 'And it shall come to pass *in the last days,* says God, That I will pour out of My Spirit on all flesh; Your sons and your daughters shall prophesy, Your young men shall see visions, Your old men shall dream dreams. And on My menservants and on My maidservants I will pour out My Spirit in those days; And they shall prophesy. *I will show wonders in heaven above And signs in the earth beneath: Blood and fire and vapor of smoke. The sun shall be turned into darkness, And the moon into blood, Before the coming of the great and awesome day of the LORD...*" (Acts 2:14-20) [emphasis mine]

What I find quite fascinating here is that Peter equates the pouring out of the Holy Spirit upon all flesh with the prophecy from Joel (and rightly so), but then he continues on to say that it is also a sign that the rest of Joel's prophecy—specifically about the "coming of the great and awesome day of the Lord"—which, as we have seen above, is all about the coming destruction of Jerusalem, is also in view.

Please also note that Peter says that these words from the prophet Joel are being fulfilled in his day; both the pouring out of the Spirit on all flesh, and the destruction marked by the Apocalyptic Hyperbole that Jesus also used to describe the events of 70 AD.

So, the reason I take the time to point all of this out to you, is that quite often Dispensationalists will try to read one of these "Day of the Lord" passages from the Old Testament and apply it to some future event like Armageddon or the day described in the book of Revelation where Jesus returns and wages war with the Nations of the earth. However, this is not how anyone else in Scripture understood these verses. Peter, and Paul and John and the other New Testament authors all equated the "Day of the Lord" with the coming destruction of the Temple.

Here are a few more New Testament applications of the "Day of the Lord" to the destruction of Jerusalem.

Paul writes to the Christians in Corinth to give them some advice about how they should respond to someone in their fellowship who is refusing to repent of some rather scandalous activity. Paul's suggestion is that should "deliver such a one to Satan for the destruction of the flesh, that his spirit may be saved in the *day of the LORD* Jesus." (1 Cor.5:5) [emphasis mine] In other words, if they won't straighten up today, perhaps it's better to see if they experience a change of heart when the "day of the Lord" comes upon them in a few short years.

In 2 Peter the author of the epistle says this:

> "But the *day of the LORD* will come *as a thief in the night,* in which the heavens will pass away with a great noise, and the elements will melt with fervent heat; both the earth and the works that are in it will be burned up." (2 Peter 3:10) [emphasis mine]

Once again, every single other reference to the "Day of the Lord" is about the destruction of Jerusalem and corresponds to what Jesus warned them about in the Olivet Discourse. However, this verse presents a problem for us in that most Bible scholars are unsure of just who wrote it and when. A great number of New Testament scholars reject the authorship of the Disciple Peter and suggest that it was most likely written long after he was already dead. So, either the epistle was written by Peter, and if so it was written prior to 67 AD when Peter was martyred, or it was written by someone else in the later second century.

If it was written by Peter, then we know that he believed the "Day of the Lord" was coming in his own lifetime as described by Jesus. If it was written by a Pseudo-Peter, then it's possible this author wasn't aware of how the "Day of the Lord" corresponded to the events described in the Olivet Discourse and therefore he may have assumed these events were still yet to come. At any rate, what should matter most to us is that every other reference we have to the "Day of the Lord" is equated in the New Testament to the events of 70 AD.

So, what have we learned? That the "Day of the Lord" prophesied all throughout the Old Testament Scriptures, and also confirmed by Jesus in the Olivet Discourse, was totally and completely fulfilled in 70 AD when the Roman Army surrounded Jerusalem and destroyed the Temple, ended the animal sacrifice and disbanded the priesthood.

Now, there is one other reference to the "Day of the Lord" we need to examine because it also holds great sway in the End Times Eschatology of today's Dispensational teachers.

THE THESSALONIAN RAPTURE?

This passage, like the 2 Peter one above, is a bit tricky for the very same reasons: Many New Testament scholars doubt whether the Apostle Paul wrote this epistle, and the dating of the book is also therefore in question. But, if we assume that Paul did write it and that it was written in his lifetime—prior to 70 AD—then we can proceed without any problem. If the book was not written by Paul but by someone else, at a later time than 70 AD, then we can only guess what this person may have thought about the things that Jesus predicted concerning the destruction of Jerusalem and this person may, or may not, have understood how these things fit together. However, since we can only speculate, let's just keep these questions in the back of our mind as we examine the text of 1 Thessalonians to see what is being communicated and see if we can make sense of it.

First, the text itself:

"For the LORD Himself will descend from heaven with a shout, with the voice of an archangel, and with the trumpet of God. And the dead in Christ will rise first. Then we who are alive and remain shall be caught up together with them in the clouds to meet the LORD in the air. And thus we shall always be with the LORD." (1 Thess. 4:16–17)

Now, I get it. This verse, taken at face value, really appears to affirm the "Left Behind" Second Coming Rapture views of the Dispensationalists. However, there's a bit more going on here than meets the eye. First, let's consider the context. If we back up a few verses, we'll see that the author wants to reassure his readers concerning those of their friends and family members in Christ who have died for their faith in Christ during the very real persecutions they were enduring at this time. Notice he says a few verses prior to this one:

"But I do not want you to be ignorant, brethren, concerning those who have fallen asleep, lest you sorrow as others who have no hope. For if we believe that Jesus died and rose again, even so God will bring with Him those who sleep in Jesus. For this we say to you by the word of the LORD, that we who are alive and remain until the coming of the LORD will by no means precede those who are asleep." (1 Thess. 4:13-15)

The authors concern is that there are those in the church in Thessalonica who have questions about the fate of those among them who have died. He writes to let them know that "those who sleep in Jesus" will be with God—and are with Him right now—and finally that those who are alive now will one day join their loved ones.

It's in this context of wanting to assuage the fears of these Christians that the author takes time to calm their hearts about the location and condition of those who have died to this point. They are safe. They are with God now and we will see them again when we ourselves meet the Lord. That's the basic point of this passage.

We might also be surprised to see just how many parallels there are between the events described in this passage, and elsewhere in the next chapter of 1 Thessalonians, and what Jesus talks about in his Olivet Discourse. Here's quick snapshot of that overlap as both make mention of:

1 THESSALONIANS	PROPHECY	MATTHEW	[3]
1 Thess. 4:16	Christ's Return	Matt. 24:30	
1 Thess. 4:16	From Heaven	Matt. 24:30	
1 Thess. 4:16	With Angels	Matt. 24:31	
1 Thess. 4:16	The Trumpet	Matt. 24:31	
1 Thess. 4:17	Believers Gathered	Matt. 24:31, 40–41	
1 Thess. 4:17	In The Clouds	Matt. 24:30	
1 Thess. 5:1–2	Timing Unknown	Matt. 24:36	
1 Thess. 5:2, 4	Comes Like A Thief	Matt. 24:43	
1 Thess. 5:3	People Unaware	Matt. 24:37–39	
1 Thess. 5:3	Compared To Birth Pains	Matt. 24:8	
1 Thess. 5:6	Believers Urged To Be Sober	Matt. 24:42	
1 Thess. 5:7	Warning Against Drunkenness	Matt. 24:49	

We might miss all of these if we don't read carefully, especially since the way Paul describes these same events is with a slightly different emphasis.

Let's read what author and Bible scholar N.T. Wright has to say about what is—and what is not—being said here:

"Paul's description of Jesus' reappearance in 1 Thessalonians 4 is a brightly colored version of what he says in two other passages. (1 Cor. 15:51–54; Phil. 3:20–2) At Jesus' 'coming' or 'appearing,' those who are still alive will be 'changed' or 'transformed' so that their mortal bodies will become incorruptible, deathless. This is all that Paul intends to say in Thessalonians, but here he borrows imagery—from biblical and political sources—to enhance his message. Little did he know how his rich metaphors would be misunderstood two millennia later.

"First, Paul echoes the story of Moses coming down the mountain with the Torah. The trumpet sounds, a loud voice is heard, and after a long wait Moses comes to see what's been going on in his absence.

"Second, he echoes Daniel 7, in which 'the people of the saints of the Most High' (that is, the 'one like a son of man') are vindicated over their pagan enemy by being raised up to sit with God in glory. This metaphor, applied to Jesus in the Gospels, is now applied to Christians who are suffering persecution.

"Third, Paul conjures up images of an emperor visiting a colony or province. The citizens go out to meet him in open country and then escort him into the city. Paul's image of the people 'meeting the Lord in the air' should be read with the assumption that the people will immediately turn around and lead the Lord back to the newly remade world.

"Paul's mixed metaphors of trumpets blowing and the living being snatched into heaven to meet the Lord are not to be understood as literal truth, as the [Dispensational] *Left Behind* series suggests, but as a vivid and biblically allusive description of the great transformation of the present world of which he speaks elsewhere." [4]

Just to make sure we understand what N.T. Wright is saying here, let's summarize this, shall we? Paul is not describing a literal appearing of Jesus in the sky one day. Even as he borrows some of what Jesus describes in his Olivet Discourse concerning the eventual destruction of Jerusalem, he also alludes to a greater truth that transcends that horrific day.

Rather than merely point to that fearful destruction event, he tries to show us a glorious reality that overshadows that dreadful "Day of the Lord" to give us a vision of a greater hope. So, he employs this extended metaphor to describe for us a spiritual reality that we can all experience today.

His allegory here is meant to emphasize our "transformation" as Jesus "appears" to us through the Holy Spirit today. The entire "transformation" experience includes not only us but also the entirety of creation itself. God is "making all things new" (See Rev. 21:5; Isa. 43:19; 65:17) and this process has already begun with the resurrection of Christ.

> RATHER THAN MERELY POINT TO THAT FEARFUL DESTRUCTION EVENT, HE TRIES TO SHOW US A GLORIOUS REALITY THAT OVERSHADOWS THAT DREADFUL "DAY OF THE LORD" TO GIVE US A VISION OF A GREATER HOPE.

This resurrection virus will eventually spread to cover all of the earth; every blade of grass, every man, woman and child, and everything in the known Universe will inevitably be transformed by the irresistible power of Christ. Even now this process is under way and it will continue until "the kingdoms of this world have become the Kingdom of our God." (Rev.11:15)

So, yes, Paul makes a reference in this passage to "the coming of the Lord" but he also uses it to metaphorically describe—in a secondary context—the ongoing transformation process that all of Creation is now undergoing. Jesus was the "first fruit" of the dead and now because of his resurrection, we are also undergoing the process of transformation into new creatures who share in the new life of Christ.

This secondary layer of Paul's teaching goes beyond the horrific details of 70 AD and illuminates the other side of the coin regarding the victory we find in Christ and the transforma-tional aspect of our abiding in Him. This will be the topic of our final section in this book, so I'll go into much more detail at that time.

For now, let's move on to the next chapter of 1 Thessalonians where Paul provides a little more detail concerning the "Day of the Lord."

> "But concerning the times and the seasons, brethren, you have no need that I should write to you. For you yourselves know perfectly that *the day of the LORD so comes as a thief in the night.* For when they say, *'Peace and safety!' then sudden destruction comes upon them,* as labor pains upon a pregnant woman. And they shall not escape. But you, brethren, are not in darkness, so that *this Day* should overtake you *as a thief.*" (1 Thess. 5:1–10) [emphasis mine]

We should note a few things about this passage. First, that the "Day of the Lord" is consistently explained as a day of destruc-tion which we already know is a reference to the events of 70 AD. Secondly, there is a reference to this day coming "like a thief" and this is significant because it appears again in this verse:

> "But the *day of the LORD* will come *as a thief in the night,* in which the heavens will pass away with a great noise, and the ele-ments will melt with fervent heat; both the earth and the works that are in it will be burned up." (2 Peter 3:10)

Once again, what's being shared here is in terms of Apocalyptic Hyperbole where references made to the heavens being removed and the earth burning up are metaphors for the physical destruc-tion of the city or nation.

But, why do both of these verses above mention that the events of this day will come like a "thief in the night"? Perhaps because Jesus used a similar phrase in his Olivet Discourse to describe these events, too:

"But understand this: *If the owner of the house had known at what time of night the thief was coming,* he would have kept watch and would not have let his house be broken into. So you also must be ready, because the Son of Man will come at an hour when you do not expect him." (Matt. 24:43–44)

Once more, all of these verses are references to the destruction of Jerusalem and the Temple. These are not referencing any Rapture or Second Coming of Christ event at some time in our future. The "coming" of the Son of Man being referenced is what happened when the things Jesus predicted in the Olivet Discourse were fulfilled in 70 AD. So, when we read these words we should always understand that they are warnings for those people who lived prior to the events of 70 AD, not to us today.

> ONCE MORE, ALL OF THESE VERSES ARE REFERENCES TO THE DESTRUCTION OF JERUSALEM AND THE TEMPLE. THESE ARE NOT REFERENCING ANY RAPTURE OR SECOND COMING OF CHRIST EVENT AT SOME TIME IN OUR FUTURE.

Hopefully this chapter has been helpful in terms of demonstrating that the events of 70 AD are described using Apocalyptic Hyperbole and that they correspond to the "Day of the Lord" passages all throughout the Old and New Testament scriptures which predict a day of fire and blood and destruction; not the Second Coming of Christ as we have often been taught.

We've also learned that the Anti-Christ is not a single person who we should expect to show up one day to fulfill some End Times prophecy, but that there were many "antichrists" according to 1 John and 2 John, respectively, and these came in the "last hour" which was also something in our past; namely the events Jesus predicted in his Olivet Discourse.

Similarly, we have learned that the Mark of the Beast was something that pointed to the Emperor Nero and not a reference to any microchip, barcode or other future banking technology that might appear in our lifetime. The Beast was Nero, not some End Times character we should expect to see before Jesus returns.

Finally, we learned that the "Rapture" passage found in 1 Thessalonians 4 is not describing a literal trumpet blast or a literal appearance of Jesus in the sky to lift Christians off the ground and defy gravity at his Second Coming, but an extended metaphor used by Paul to describe the "coming of the Lord" in the context of the transformational power of His resurrection which will one day "make all things new" as promised throughout Scripture.

Before we move on to fully unpacking this "slow-motion second coming of Christ" concept, we have one final question to answer concerning the book of Revelation and what it is—and what it isn't—all about.

This is what we'll examine in our next chapter.

CHAPTER 8

HOW SHOULD WE READ REVELATION?

"As a child growing up in church... I assumed [Revelation] was... some kind of un-deciphered code about the end times [and] a veiled foretelling of the geopolitical events of the late twentieth century. But I was mistaken."

— BRIAN ZAHND[1]

For most Christians, the book of Revelation is veiled in mystery. We're not exactly sure what everything we read in this book about dragons, beasts, bottomless pits and floating cities is all about, but we're fairly confident of one thing: *It's about something that is going to happen in the future, at the end of time.*

Why do we think this? Well, to be very honest because this is pretty much what we're told from the moment we're handed a Bible. If you want to know how everything ends, they tell us, just turn to the back of the book to find out. But, is that really what Revelation is all about? Why don't we look at the book for ourselves and see what it has to say about why it was written, to whom it was written, and when the fantastic events it describes are supposed to take place. Shall we?

From the very opening of the book we read that this testimony is "The revelation of Jesus Christ, which God gave him to show his servants what must soon take place." (Rev. 1:1)

Please notice, the very first verse tells us that the events we are about to read about "*must soon take place.*" So, why should we expect that these things are yet to come to pass? We are reading this book almost two thousand years later. Are we seriously going to believe that this book of Revelation is still unfulfilled today?

Let me humbly suggest that we take verse 1 of chapter 1 at face value. This "revelation of Jesus Christ" is about things that, for the author, "*must soon take place*" and as we shall see, they most certainly did take place in the months and years after it was written.

By this time, you should already have a fairly good idea about what I'm going to show you next. This book of Revelation—like the Olivet Discourse and the "Day of the Lord" references we've previously examined—is primarily aimed at making sense of a particular point in the history of the Jewish people and the early Christian Church: The destruction of Jerusalem and the Temple in 70 AD.

Revelation is also about how Jesus is Lord and Caesar is not. As author Brian Zahnd explains it:

> "The book of Revelation was written around the end of the first century, and is a prophetic critique of the Roman Empire. It's a daring proclamation that Jesus Christ is the world's new Emperor. Revelation is a wild and creative portrayal of the conflict between the beastly empire of Rome and the peaceable reign of the Lamb of God. What it foretells is the eventual triumph of the kingdom of Christ. It does this in a genre

of macabre comedy—hideous monsters finally conquered by a little Lamb, a slaughtered Lamb who lives again. This is how John the Revelator tells of the triumph of Jesus over the Roman Empire and all beastly empires to come.

"After riding the peace donkey on Palm Sunday to contrast his peaceable kingdom with the violent empires of a pagan world, Jesus does not later [in Revelation] contradict himself by riding a war-horse in an exaggerated imitation of Genghis Khan... Jesus is ever and always the slaughtered Lamb... Christ always rules from the cross... John stresses that Jesus reigns through self-sacrifice by depicting the white horse's rider as wearing a robe drenched in blood *before* the battle begins. Jesus' robe is soaked in his own blood. Jesus doesn't shed the blood of his enemies; Jesus sheds his own blood. This is the gospel! The rider on the white horse is the slaughtered Lamb, not the slaughtering beast... the sword the rider uses to smite the nations is not in his hand but in his mouth... this is not Caesar's sword but the word of God... Jesus wages war by self-sacrifice and by what he says. Jesus combats evil by co-suffering love and the word of God... A fallen world addicted to war does not believe this, but the followers of Jesus do, or should! If Jesus conquers evil by killing his enemies, he's just another Caesar. But the whole point of John's Revelation is that Jesus is *nothing* like Caesar."[2]

So, if we keep this in mind whenever we read Revelation it should help us to understand that much of what we're seeing in these fantastic metaphors is on the level of a farce. The Great Dragon and the Beast are instantly defeated by a tiny lamb. The Lord Jesus enters the great Battle of Armageddon covered in his own blood before the fight even begins. He's holding the sword in his mouth, not in his hands because it is the message of the Gospel that metaphorically "kills" our enemies by making them our friends.

One of my favorite examples of this sort of thing is when we are told about the "Wrath of the Lamb" in Revelation. As my friend Richard Murray notes:

"Jesus is the Lamb of God. So He, by extension, is the wrath of God personified [in Revelation 6:16]. But here is the thing: Lambs have no wrath.

"So, the term is an oxymoron. It's an image clash where wrath itself is deconstructed by the jarring contradiction of two incompatible terms. This then allows divine wrath to be conceptually recast as the restorative and curative energies of God. Hence the Lamb.

"So let's look at both God's birth statement and death statement regarding Jesus as the revelation of 'the wrath of God.'

"Here is the divine wrath statement given by angelic pronouncement at His birth: 'Peace on earth, goodwill to man.' (Luke 2:14) Hmmm.

"And here is His bookend statement on the issue of wrath at His death: 'Forgive them Father, for they know not what they do.' (Luke 23:34) Hmmm.

"The 'wrath of the Lamb' is now revealed. Peace, goodwill, and forgiveness toward all men!"[3]

This same oxymoron is further exemplified in David Bentley Hart's translation of the New Testament where he notes that the "Lamb" in Revelation 5:6 is more accurately rendered as "The suckling lamb", which is the equivalent of a kitten or a newborn puppy.

As Hart puts it:

"Not arnos or arnen—a 'lamb'—but an arnion—literally, a 'little lamb' or 'lambkin', a term most properly applied to a lamb that is still nursing." [4]

So, this image of Christ as the "suckling lamb" or "newborn lambkin" further challenges the notion that the "wrath of the Lamb" is anything other than an intentionally jarring mashup of clashing ideas that should lead us to rethink our notions of the Wrath of God.

Are you terrified at the notion of enraging a kitten? Do you tremble at the thought of falling under the fearsome wrath of a puppy? Of course not. This is exactly why John uses such language in Revelation; to emphasize the ridiculousness of the notion that anyone should ever fear the Wrath of the Baby Lamb. Lambs have no wrath. This is the very point he wants us to understand.

> ARE YOU TERRIFIED AT THE NOTION OF ENRAGING A KITTEN? DO YOU TREMBLE AT THE THOUGHT OF FALLING UNDER THE FEARSOME WRATH OF A PUPPY? OF COURSE NOT.

We see this sort of subversive imagery all through the book of Revelation. It's very intentional. It's meant to make us stop and think. But we should never take these wild images and surreal depictions of seven-headed dragons and scorpion-tailed horses literally. The imaginary nature of these things is meant to prevent us from seeing them as literal. We are invited to see them and understand them as metaphors for deeper realities that lie behind the images.

It's when we fail to see these images as symbols that we get into the most trouble. This is one of the central mistakes made by Darby and those who follow his Futurist End Times narrative. They see everything as literally real and get confused by these symbols. In the process they totally miss the deeper meaning the author intends to communicate through these symbols. Once again, Brian Zahnd provides an excellent analogy for us to consider:

> "We must remember that everything in Revelation is told in the language of symbol... But these symbols point to glorious and terrible realities. One of our challenges is that we are 2,000 years removed from the origin of these symbols.

> "Today, if we see a cartoon of a donkey and an elephant wearing boxing gloves, we recognize it as a comic commentary on American politics. But it would likely be hard for someone

2,000 years from now to discern this political meaning. So keep in mind that most of the monstrous images in Revelation are symbols for cosmic evil working through the Roman Empire.

"But it's most important to remember what Revelation is, and what it isn't. It's *not* a coded newspaper foretelling geopolitical events of the 21st century. It *is* a glorious revelation of the triumph of Jesus Christ. Jesus' lamb-like kingdom brings a saving alternative to the beast-like empires of the world. Revelation doesn't anticipate the end of God's good creation—it anticipates the end of violent empire." [5] [emphasis mine]

The book of Revelation, then, is less a story about how Jesus will return in the sky one day riding on a white horse to slaughter millions of sinners and establish his everlasting Kingdom on earth and more about the story of how Jesus has *already* vanquished the Roman Empire by the power of His Gospel and the testimony of the early Christians (See Rev.12:11), which also included their death at the hands of those who persecuted them.

> REVELATION IS A STORY OF HOW THE FOOLISHNESS OF GOD IS GREATER THAN THE WISDOM OF MEN. IT'S A STORY OF HOW THE WEAK THINGS OF GOD OVERCOME THE POWERFUL FORCES OF DARKNESS.

Revelation is a story of how the foolishness of God is greater than the wisdom of men. It's a story of how the weak things of God overcome the powerful forces of darkness. It's also the story of how baby Lambs slay Great Dragons, and how those who die live forever and how even the enemies of God are shown great mercy. (See Rev.22:2; 17)

So, while the vast majority of what we read in Revelation is intended to be about events that—in John's time frame—"must soon take place", and were fulfilled in 70 AD, there are portions of the book that are indeed about something we are currently experiencing today and can expect to see happen in the future.

However, it's not something that the average Christian has any clue about and almost no one ever emphasizes when it comes to the book of Revelation or the implications of the "Second Coming" of Christ to the world.

This last section of our book will endeavor to explain this little-known aspect of Biblical Eschatology and hopefully allow us to re-imagine our idea of what it means to think about the Return of Christ in these last days.

I hope you're ready for what's next. It's going to require you to shift your paradigm and re-think almost everything you thought you knew about the idea of the future rule and reign of Christ on earth and how we should interpret those scriptures that speak about the Second Coming of Jesus.

Don't say I didn't warn you.

CHAPTER 9

THE SLOW-MOTION SECOND COMING OF CHRIST

"What I don't understand about these Left Behind books is how there can be so f---ing many of them, given that their subject is Armageddon. How long can a writer drag out the Second Coming? Even a trilogy would be a stretch, but ten novels going on eleven, all huge sellers, with no final volume in sight? I smell a con."

— WALTER KIRN, AUTHOR OF *UP IN THE AIR* [1]

In the quote above, taken from an article in *GQ* magazine, Walter Kirn shares his candid take on the Dispensational End Times narrative and nails what makes it all so hard to believe: the fact that it's like an endless "coming soon" trailer for a film that never arrives in theaters, and yet continually sells tickets that break the box office year after year, without ever delivering the goods.

But he also puts his finger on another point that I want us to recognize; the fact that this version of the Apocalypse is so fascinating and endlessly marketable that, once we expose it as a fraud it leaves a gaping hole that is almost impossible to fill. Quoting from Kirn's article once more we read:

"… [According to the Futurists] the End of the World is never ending, because it's the only dramatic game in town. Drop the curtain on the Apocalypse and there are no more stories—the party's over. Which means [books like] the *Art of Desecration*, and the Christian thriller in general, is the art of the stall—of giving the reader a sense of forward motion without moving things any closer to a conclusion. This task is complicated by the fact that the genre's basic principles rule out new suspense. Since the heroes are assured of going to Heaven, it doesn't really matter if they die, and since the villains are bound to burn in hell, it doesn't matter if they win. Which they won't, of course. The Bible tells us so." [2]

This is my personal challenge. Once I expose the fact that the Dispensational End Times narrative is essentially a hoax perpetrated on the Christian world in 1830 by John Nelson Darby, the hardest thing to do is to give anyone a story that is equally compelling, bombastic and thrilling as the one created by Darby and his disciples.

I mean, if I manage to convince people that the version of the End Times we've been told is a fairy tale and I take away everyone's notion of a one world government ruled by a demon-ically-possessed Anti-Christ who rebuilds the Temple, unleashes fantastic creatures from the Abyss, forces everyone to take the Mark of the Beast and goes to war with Jesus who flies down out of the sky on a white horse with a massive sword shooting out of his mouth in the war to end all wars, what in the world could possibly top, or replace, a block-busting cataclysmic epic story like that? Is such a thing even possible?

Probably not. But hopefully I don't need to invent a better story than the one Darby invented. Hopefully all I need to do is to show everyone what the Bible actually does say about the Second Coming of Christ and what our role in this End Times narrative truly looks like. It might not be as cinematic and explosively jaw-dropping as Darby's script, but it could be the most mind-bending twist in the story that no one saw coming and takes everyone by complete surprise.

IT MIGHT NOT BE AS CINEMATIC AND EXPLOSIVELY JAW-DROPPING AS DARBY'S SCRIPT, BUT IT COULD BE THE MOST MIND-BENDING TWIST IN THE STORY THAT NO ONE SAW COMING AND TAKES EVERYONE BY COMPLETE SURPRISE.

To me, that's what I think the actual Second Coming of Jesus is really all about. It's an unexpected plot twist that is hidden in plain sight for everyone to see and once we discover this secret code I think it could be like taking the red pill and waking up in our pod as we make our escape from the Matrix that has held us captive for so long.

As a quick reminder, the Dispensational Futurist version of the End Times and the Second Coming assures us that—one day very soon—Jesus is about to crack the sky wide open, whoop his enemies in a massive battle, rapture us into Heaven (depending on who's telling the story), and destroy the earth with fire, only to create a New Heaven and a New Earth where we all live happily ever after (at least, the Christians do).

The problem with this End Times story—other than the fact that the Bible never teaches any of this—is that it basically keeps us in an endless pause mode as we wait for Jesus to come back and fix everything. Because we are always being assured that this Second Coming is about to happen (probably in our lifetime), we tend to kick back and wait for Jesus to show up and make it all better.

Now, there are dozens of verses in the Scriptures that tell us *not* to sit back and wait and even warn us not to be found idly asleep at the wheel when Jesus comes back, (see Matt. 24:42; 1 Thess. 5:6), and many Christians will even deny that they think this way, but in my experience those who take a Futurist view of the End Times tend to use the phrase "Jesus is going to come back and destroy the earth soon anyway so why bother to save it now?" quite frequently.

UNLESS WE WAKE UP FROM THIS SLUMBER AND SHAKE OFF THE COBWEBS, THE BODY OF CHRIST WILL REMAIN LARGELY MOTIONLESS AND LIFELESS LIKE AN UN-RESURRECTED JESUS WHO IS STILL IN THE DARK OF THE TOMB WITH THE STONE ROLLED OVER THE DOOR.

This "Coming Soon" version of the End Times paralyzes the modern Christian and keeps them in a constant state of waiting for a Second Coming that never comes, and while we wait the world is dying and suffering endlessly.

Unless we wake up from this slumber and shake off the cobwebs, the Body of Christ will remain largely motionless and lifeless like an un-resurrected Jesus who is still in the dark of the tomb with the stone rolled over the door.

But, what if we took another perspective? What if we could re-think this whole "Second Coming" idea and see a new possibility hidden in the scriptures?

For example, if I were to ask you, "What is it that all of Creation is awaiting eagerly?" You might be tempted to say, "The return of Jesus!" And you would be wrong.

See, what Paul says is that all Creation is waiting eagerly for those who are in Christ to awaken and rise up.

> "For *the creation waits in eager expectation for the children of God to be revealed.* For the creation was subjected to frustration, not by its own choice, but by the will of the one who subjected it, *in hope that the creation itself will be liberated from its bondage to decay and brought into the freedom and glory of the children of God.*" (Romans 8:19–21) [emphasis mine]

So, all of Creation is eagerly awaiting the Body of Christ—that's us—to wake up and bring forth the Kingdom of God, which lies within each of us. Like tiny seeds of mustard pressed into the dry ground or a light sprinkling of yeast that spreads within the lump of dough, we are the promise of a Kingdom to come that all Creation yearns for.

This has always been part of the Father's Master Plan—to transform us so that we can transform the kingdoms of this world into the Kingdom of God.

> "The kingdoms of this world are become the kingdoms of our LORD, and of his Christ; and he shall reign for ever and ever." (Revelation 11:15)

So, let's please forget about "winning America back for God." Our mission is much greater than this. Our mission and purpose is to usher in the Eternal Kingdom of Christ—where His perfect will is always accomplished in the lives of His people—and to transform others around us into subversive agents who are also carrying around the seed of the Kingdom within.

It's not about turning America into a nation where Christians feel more comfortable and "at home." It's about changing people into transformational agents of the Kingdom who are radiating love, joy, peace, patience, kindness, goodness, mercy and perseverance.

Just before this passage in Romans about how "all Creation is groaning," Paul says something wonderful about our identity in Christ as "Children of God":

> "For those who are led by the Spirit of God are the children of God. The Spirit you received does not make you slaves, so that you live in fear again; rather, the Spirit you received brought about your adoption to son-ship. And by him we cry, 'Abba, Father.' The Spirit himself testifies with our spirit that we are God's children. Now if we are children, then we are heirs—heirs of God and co-heirs with Christ, if indeed we share in his sufferings in order that we may also share in his glory." (Romans 8: 14–17)

Please notice that, as the Children of God, we are:

- "Led by the Spirit"

- "Without fear"

- "Heirs of God"

- "Co-heirs with Christ"

- "Sharing in the sufferings and the glory of Jesus"

In fact, it is this process of suffering that is key to what Paul is saying in this passage. This is why he says:

"I consider that our present sufferings are not worth comparing with the glory that will be revealed in us." (v. 18)

Note that Paul does not say that our sufferings don't compare to Heaven, or to a place we will go when Jesus comes back. Nope. Look again. Paul says:

"Our present sufferings are not worth comparing with the *glory that will be revealed in us*." [emphasis mine]

What is this glory that will be revealed in us? It's the very same glory that Paul says *"all creation waits in eager expectation for"* when *"the children of God are revealed,"* so he encourages us to endure suffering in this life, because through that suffering for the Kingdom and the Gospel of Jesus, we are being transformed into His image and we are fulfilling our call as seeds and as yeast to usher in the glorious Kingdom of God in the here and now.

THIS MEANS WE ARE NOT WAITING FOR JESUS TO COME BACK AND FIX ANYTHING. NOT AT ALL.

Therefore, all creation is groaning for you and me to wake up, step out, and begin to live as citizens of the Kingdom of God at this very moment in time.

This means we are not waiting for Jesus to come back and fix anything. Not at all. Instead, we are recognizing our identity in Christ and awakening to our calling to be the Incarnation of Christ in the world today.

RE-THINKING THE SECOND COMING

So, if all Creation is groaning and waiting for us to wake up and continue the work of Jesus in the world, then what is it we are waiting for, if anything?

Well, if we're honest, most of us are waiting for Jesus to return, at least in some form. We want to see his face, we want to hear his voice, we want to stand beside him and to walk with him and to experience him in the flesh. These are beautiful desires and I wouldn't want to take this away from anyone.

But what if you could experience all of these things right here and now? I mean, what if the "Second Coming" has in some ways already taken place and you're just not aware of it yet?

What many of us don't realize is that the Greek word that we often find translated in our English Bibles as the *"coming of Christ"* is *"Parousia"* which appears 24 times throughout the New Testament. What this word literally means is, "Divine Presence" or "Nearness." Several times the word is generically applied to the nearness or presence of one person to another.

So, let's keep in mind that when the term is used in connection with Christ, it literally is speaking about the "nearness" or "presence" of Christ, not at all about physical appearance of Jesus in the sky.

The problem we have is that whenever we read the English phrase "the coming of Christ" there's a little movie that plays in our imagination and it is the one we inherited from Darby where Jesus is coming back in the sky on the white horse. But, what if we imagined this as speaking of the physical presence of Christ with us here and now instead? And what if this is really what Jesus wanted us to imagine all along?

Turn back to the Gospel of John and notice what Jesus says to his disciples just before the crucifixion:

> "Now I am going to him who sent me, yet none of you asks me 'Where are you going?' Because I have said these things, you are filled with grief. But I tell you the truth: It is for your good [or 'It is better for you'] that I am going away." (John 16:5–6)

ACCORDING TO JESUS, IT WAS AND IS "BETTER" FOR US IF HE GOES AWAY. BUT WE DON'T BELIEVE THAT. IN FACT, MOST OF US INSIST THAT IT WILL BE SO MUCH BETTER WHEN JESUS COMES BACK AGAIN.

According to Jesus, it was and is "better" for us if he goes away. But we don't believe that. In fact, most of us insist that it will be so much better when Jesus comes back again. However, if we understand God's plan from the beginning, we can hopefully begin to accept what Jesus tells us and finally believe that it really is better for us that Jesus went away. Why? Because Jesus assures us that it's only when he goes away that the Holy Spirit can come and fill each and every one of us:

> "But I tell you the truth, it is to your advantage that I go away; for if I do not go away, the Helper will not come to you; but if I go, I will send Him to you... But when He, the Spirit of truth, comes, He will guide you into all the truth; for He will not speak on His own initiative, but whatever He hears, He will speak; and He will disclose to you what is to come. He will glorify Me, for He will take of Mine and will disclose it to you. All things that the Father has are Mine; therefore I said that He takes of Mine and will disclose it to you. (John 16:7–15)

Jesus also says something earlier in John's Gospel about what will happen after he goes away and about when he comes back. Most of us are quite familiar with this verse, but I think we may have missed the entire meaning of what Jesus is trying to tell us here. First, let's read what he says in Chapter 14 of John:

> "Do not let your heart be troubled; believe in God, believe also in Me. In My Father's house are many dwelling places; if it were not so, I would have told you; for I go to prepare a place for you. *If I go and prepare a place for you, I will come again and receive you to Myself, that where I am, there you may be also.* And you know the way where I am going." Thomas said to Him, "LORD, we do not know where You are going, how do we know the way?" Jesus said to him, "I am the way, and the truth, and the life; no one comes to the Father but through Me." (John 14:1–6) [emphasis mine]

Most of my life I've understood this verse as being about Heaven. But eventually I started to notice that the phrase "my Father's house" is used by Jesus exclusively throughout the other Gospels to refer to the Temple.

For example, early on in Luke when Jesus is separated from his parents for three days they find him teaching in the Temple. When they finally find him Jesus says, "Didn't you know I would be in my Father's house?" (Luke 2:48–50) Also, when Jesus clears the Temple of those who sell doves he declares, "Stop making My Father's house a place of business." (John 2:15–17)

This makes a lot of sense in context as well if we look at what Jesus is speaking to His disciples about in this section of the Gospel of John. We find it's all about what's going to happen next, how to prepare for the coming persecution, etc.

So, if Jesus is speaking about the Temple here, and not about Heaven, then we need to try to re-read this section with new eyes. For one thing, the term "the Temple of God" is re-defined throughout the New Testament as the Church, or the Body of Christ. Why? Because, as we have seen several times already, the physical Temple in Jerusalem was bound to be destroyed. And we've also seen that the End Times Temple that Jesus came to establish was us—the Temple of God not made by human hands.

Therefore, I think what Jesus is teaching His disciples when he says: "In My Father's house are many rooms (dwelling places)" is that, in the Temple (which is now the Church) there is room for many people.

Throughout the New Testament, the Apostles talk about "dwelling places" where we (the people of God) find rest in our Lord and Savior. For instance:

> "If anyone has my words and obeys me… we will come and make our house (dwelling place) with them." (John 14:23)

The very same word Jesus uses here for "house" is also the same as in the passage about the "many dwelling places" in His "Father's house" above.

> "Christ is the LORD over his own house, whose house we are if we hold fast our confidence and the boast of our hope firm until the end." (Hebrews 3:6)

So, the idea that we, the Church, are now God's "dwelling place" is all through the New Testament. Got it? Ok, let's continue to look at the rest of the passage:

> "If it were not so, I would have told you; for I go to prepare a place for you."(v.2)

Here, I believe, Jesus is telling His disciples that He needs to go—to get out of the way—in order to make room for them (the Church) to grow as He has promised.

> "If I go and prepare a place for you, I will come again and receive you to Myself, that where I am, there you may be also."(v.3)

Jesus says that if He goes away, it will make room (prepare a place) for the disciples. He also says that he does this so that where he is they will be also. Where is He going? To be with the Father. Now, notice what Jesus says about those who love him:

"If anyone loves Me, he will keep My word; *and My Father will love him, and We will come to him and make Our abode [dwelling] with him.*" (John 14:23) [emphasis mine]

So, where does God dwell? In us—His Church. His Temple. We are His "Father's House." This household of God is the Church:

"I write so that you will know how one ought to conduct himself *in the household of God, which is the church of the living God,* the pillar and support of the truth." (1 Timothy 3:15) [emphasis mine]

"So then you are no longer strangers and aliens, but *you are fellow citizens with the saints, and are of God's household.*" (Ephesians 2:18-20) [emphasis mine]

"*You also, as living stones, are being built up as a spiritual house* for a holy priesthood, to offer up spiritual sacrifices acceptable to God through Jesus Christ." (1 Peter 2:4–6) [emphasis mine]

This promise of Jesus to go away in order to prepare a place for the Temple to expand into the "many rooms" or "dwelling places" was fulfilled at Pentecost when Peter was filled with the Holy Spirit and preached the Gospel of the Kingdom and thousands followed Christ in that day. And this promise is still ongoing right now.

So, it may be that Jesus isn't promising us "mansions in Heaven" after all. In fact, most of the scriptures indicate that our eternal destination is to live here, on a New Earth, and reign with Christ forever.

> **SO, IT MAY BE THAT JESUS ISN'T PROMISING US "MANSIONS IN HEAVEN" AFTER ALL. IN FACT, MOST OF THE SCRIPTURES INDICATE THAT OUR ETERNAL DESTINATION IS TO LIVE HERE, ON A NEW EARTH, AND REIGN WITH CHRIST FOREVER.**

"Now the dwelling of God is with men, and he will live with them. They will be his people, and God himself will be with them and be their God." (Revelation 21:1–3)

Now, if we put all of this together here's what we can see: Jesus promised that he would go away and that it was better for us if he did. This was so that the Holy Spirit could be poured out on all flesh. In this way, Jesus is now always with each and every one of us; every day, all the time. Not only that, Jesus promised that, if he went away, he would make a place that where he was, there we could be with him, too. So, did Jesus go away? Yes, he did. What did he do when he went away? He created a place where we could dwell with him and with the Father. Now, this is where it starts to get interesting. What did Jesus say he was going to do after he went away? He said this:

> "And if I go and prepare a place for you, I will come back and take you with me so that you may also be where I am." (John 14:3)

Did you see it? Jesus went away. We know that. He prepared a place for us. We know that too. And if Jesus went away and if he prepared a place for us, he said that he would come back and take us with him. Therefore, Jesus has already left and come back. How do we know? Because he said that he would come back *"so that you may also be where I am."*

So, where does Jesus tell us that he and the Father are dwelling right now? He says that they have made their home in us. What's more, Jesus has also told us that he would never leave us or forsake us. In fact, one of the Messianic names of Jesus is "Emmanuel" which means "God with us!", so how can Jesus come back if he promised never to leave us and if he's already made his home inside of us?

In fact, this is exactly what the New Covenant promise has always been about. God has always forecasted his desire to establish a reality where he would dwell with us and know us intimately:

> *"This is the new covenant I will make with the people of Israel*
>   *after that time," declares the* LORD.
> "I will put my law in their minds
>   and write it on their hearts.
> I will be their God,
>   and they will be my people.
> No longer will they teach their neighbor,
>   or say to one another, 'Know the* LORD,'
> because they will all know me,
>   from the least of them to the greatest,"
>   declares the LORD.
> "For I will forgive their wickedness
>   and will remember their sins no more."
>
> (Jeremiah 31:33–34) [emphasis mine]

So, if Jeremiah prophesied that this New Covenant would be proclaimed, and if Jesus already announced it as coming "in his blood" in the upper room (Luke 22:20), and if the terms of this New Covenant are that:

- God will put His law in our hearts

- God will be our God and we will be His people

- Everyone will now have access to knowing God personally

- God will forgive their sins and remember them no more

Then the bottom line is this: The New Covenant reality is here, right now, today.

What this means is that we are now the Temple of the Living God where He dwells within every one of us. As Paul puts it:

> "For we are the temple of the living God. As God has said: "I will live with them and walk among them, and I will be their God, and they will be my people." (2 Cor. 6:18)

Notice that Paul here directly ties this statement about us being God's temple with the fulfillment of the New Covenant promise *"I will be their God and they will be my people."* So, all of this is true, right now.

So, when Peter writes about the "Day of the Lord" coming when the old creation will be destroyed by fire and the new heavens and the new earth will be established, this is exactly what he is referring to: The end of the Old Covenant and the establishment of the New Covenant. This is why Peter ends that statement by saying:

> "...That day will bring about the destruction of the heavens by fire, and the elements will melt in the heat. But in keeping with his promise, *we are looking forward to a new heaven and a new earth, where righteousness dwells.*" (2 Peter 3:13) [emphasis mine]

The good news is this: The old things have passed away. The new has come. As Paul puts it:

> "Therefore, if anyone is in Christ, *the new creation has come: The old has gone, the new is here!*" (2 Cor. 5:17) [emphasis mine]

I know this may be difficult to take in all at once, but hopefully you can begin to wrap your brain around the fact that we are living, right now, today, in the New Heaven and the New Earth where God has made His dwelling among men and women.

Don't believe me? Read this passage from Revelation again and let me know if there's anything here that hasn't already been fulfilled in our day:

> "Then I saw a new heaven and a new earth, for the first heaven and the first earth had passed away, and there was no longer any sea. I saw the Holy City, the New Jerusalem, coming down out of heaven from God, prepared as a bride beautifully dressed for her husband. And I heard a loud voice from the throne saying, "Now the dwelling of God is with men, and he will live with

them. They will be his people, and God himself will be with them and be their God." (Revelation 21:1–3)

Now, we may argue that this has not literally taken place because there is still the first heaven and the first earth. We still have an ocean on our planet. So, this can't be reality yet. Or can it?

Remember the verse in 2 Peter we just looked at? Notice how it speaks about 70 AD as being "the destruction of the heavens by fire, and the elements will melt in the heat"? We already talked about that use of Apocalyptic Hyperbole to describe cataclysmic events being figurative, not literal. So, when we read Revelation 21 above let's keep this in mind and recognize that it's talking about what happens after 70 AD—when the sky is rolled back as a scroll and the end of the age comes with fire and blood, etc.—and what comes next is the reality we are now part of today: The Bride of Christ—that's the Church—is now the place where God dwells with men. This is the fulfillment of the New Covenant promise Jesus made with us. We are living in this reality now.

Jesus wanted us to grasp this truth. The Dispensationalists want us to wait for a series of events to play out in the Middle East before we can begin to experience these things, but the Gospels and the rest of the New Testament tells us another story—We are already knee deep in the fulfillment of the End Times and most of us don't even realize it.

THE DISPENSATIONALISTS WANT US TO WAIT FOR A SERIES OF EVENTS TO PLAY OUT IN THE MIDDLE EAST BEFORE WE CAN BEGIN TO EXPERIENCE THESE THINGS, BUT THE GOSPELS AND THE REST OF THE NEW TESTAMENT TELLS US ANOTHER STORY—WE ARE ALREADY KNEE DEEP IN THE FULFILLMENT OF THE END TIMES AND MOST OF US DON'T EVEN REALIZE IT.

As John predicted in Revelation 21:1–3, the New Jerusalem has replaced the Old Jerusalem. This city is now composed of people who are in Christ. We are the Bride of Christ. His home is now among us. He is our God. We are His people. We can all know Him directly, right now.

We are the End Times Temple. There's no need to build one in Jerusalem. We are the New Jerusalem that comes down from God out of Heaven. There's no need to wait for that to happen. We are the place that Jesus went away to prepare so that where he is we may be also.

If Heaven is defined as the place where God dwells, then let's take a moment to remind ourselves where that actually is.

We aren't waiting to go to Heaven. We already carry Heaven around with us every moment of every day. We aren't waiting for Jesus to appear because he has made his home in us already. We're not waiting for Jesus to come and fix anything in this world because we now understand that we are his hands and his feet and his voice and his heart walking around on the earth today.

WHERE IS JESUS RIGHT NOW?

What we have failed to understand is that Jesus is already alive and at work on planet earth right now. His "Parousia" (Second Coming) has been accomplished by the outpouring of His Holy Spirit on all flesh as recorded in Acts 2.

Today, every single one of us is filled with the presence ("Parousia") of Christ. In this way, Christ is now here and we are the Incarnation of Christ to the world. Instead of one Christ expressed through the person of Jesus, we are now members of a worldwide Body of Christ which incarnates the presence of Christ all around the globe.

FILLED WITH THE FULLNESS OF CHIRST

There are three scriptures that may help us wrap our minds around the idea that Christ has already come in the flesh (ours) and how this concept is to be understood. First, let's look at what the author of Colossians says about the superlative identity of Christ:

> "*The Son is the image of the invisible God, the firstborn over all creation.* For in him all things were created: things in heaven and on earth, visible and invisible, whether thrones or powers or rulers or authorities; all things have been created through him and for him. He is before all things, and in him all things hold together. And he is the head of the body, the church; he is the beginning and the firstborn from among the dead, so that in everything he might have the supremacy. *For God was pleased to have all his fullness dwell in him, and through him to reconcile to himself all things, whether things on earth or things in heaven, by making peace through his blood, shed on the cross.*" (Col. 1:15–20) [emphasis mine]

First, we notice that Jesus is "the image of the invisible God." This corresponds to other scriptures throughout the New Testament like Hebrews 1 where we're told that Jesus is "the radiance of God's glory and the exact representation of His being, sustaining all things by his powerful word." (Heb.1:3) But, the second part is almost unbearably amazing where we read how: *"God was pleased to have all his fullness dwell in him."*

Now, you need to hang on to that concept long enough to read what is said in this verse:

> "For *in Christ all the fullness of the Deity lives in bodily form, and in Christ you have been brought to fullness.* He is the head over every power and authority. "(Col. 2:9–10) [emphasis mine]

There it is again: Christ embodies all the fullness of God, but it's the next part that knocks me backward: *"…and in Christ, you have been brought to fullness."*

Are you ready for the next part? Here it is:

"And God placed all things under his [Christ's] feet and appointed him to be head over everything for the church, which is *his body, the fullness of him who fills everything in every way.*" (Eph. 1:22–23) [emphasis mine]

This one might be a bit harder to notice because of the way Paul composes his thoughts, but essentially this verse says:

- God placed everything under Christ's feet.

- Christ is the head over everything for the Church.

- The Church is His Body.

- The Church is the fullness of Christ.

- Christ fills everything in every way.

So… if we put all of these verses together we end up with something like this:

- Christ embodies the fullness of God.

- We, in Christ, are brought to that same fullness.

- Christ, who fills everything in every way, fills us with His fullness.

What does this mean? To be quite honest, I think it means more things than I have the capacity to express in words. What I think I can say is that Christ is not merely the "image of God." Christ is filled with the entire fullness of God. Not only this: But the entire fullness of God is contained "in bodily form."

Does that make any sense? The Infinite is contained within a finite human body? Well, that is what it says. But then we learn that *we* are now Christ's body and that *we* are now "brought to fullness" and *we* are "the fullness of Him who fills everything in every way."

[Insert sound of mind exploding here]

So, let's try to follow this if we can. First, the fullness of God was contained in Christ's body. Now, we are Christ's body. That means that all the fullness of God still lives in bodily form today. Where? In us. You and me: The new Incarnation of Christ.

Not a little bit of Christ. Not a residue of the Divine. We are talking *the fullness of God*, alive in us—in bodily form.

This means that God is alive, in you and me, right now. The very same way that God was alive in Christ, He is now alive in us. The total, one hundred percent, absolute fullness of the living God is now alive within humanity!

> THIS MEANS THAT GOD IS ALIVE, IN YOU AND ME, RIGHT NOW. THE VERY SAME WAY THAT GOD WAS ALIVE IN CHRIST, HE IS NOW ALIVE IN US.

As amazing as this may be, it is totally consistent with everything else we read in the Gospels and the New Testament.

"By this, love is perfected with us, so that we may have confidence in the Day of Judgment; because as He is, so also are we in this world." (1 Jn. 4:17)

"Abide in me and I [Jesus] will abide in you." (John 15:4)

WHAT ABOUT THE FUTURE RESURRECTION?

From those who doubt this perspective there comes the question about the promised resurrection of the dead which is often alluded to in prophetic scriptures in connection with the future return of Christ. This is a valid question we need to respond to, so I'll take a few moments to examine it here.

The argument that there is a future resurrection event still to come, prior to the Second Coming of Christ, is founded in these verses, with emphasis added:

> "Then I saw thrones, and they sat on them, and judgment was given to them. And I saw *the souls of those who had been beheaded* because of their testimony of Jesus and because of the word of God, and those who had not worshiped the beast or his image, and had not received the mark on their forehead and on their hand; *and they came to life and reigned with Christ for a thousand years.* The rest of the dead did not come to life until the thousand years were completed. *This is the first resurrection.* Blessed and holy is *the one who has a part in the first resurrection;* over these the second death has no power…" (Rev. 20:4–6) [emphasis mine]

Let's start by looking at this passage in Revelation. The only problem this verse presents to us is if we take these things literally. As you might guess, it's not a good idea to take almost anything we read in the book of Revelation as literal, given the nature of Apocalyptic Hyperbole used all throughout this book of symbol and metaphor. However, we can see a few clues in this passage about what is meant by "resurrection" and how it might fit into our eschatology.

First, we notice that it is "the souls of those who had been beheaded" who John says "came to life and reigned with Christ for a thousand years." These people are identified specifically as "those who had not worshipped the beast or his image, and had not received the mark [of the Beast]." So, we're talking about every Christian who was alive at the time of the writing of John's Revelation text; the very people who were, in that moment, being persecuted for their faith in Christ. What does John tell them? That their reward for resisting Nero's intense persecutions would be this: they would experience the resurrection into new life and reign with Christ. When? After they died. How do know this? Because, once again, John says it is "the souls of those who have been beheaded" by Nero who experience this.

For the record, this is in line with everything we see taught in the rest of the scriptures about the resurrection. Paul affirms to us that we are now already "raised with Christ" and "seated with Christ in the heavenly places" (See Eph.2:4–6), which is the exact thing John says happens to these Christians in Rev. 20 above. They are resurrected with Christ and they reign with Him. We also experience this right now.

We should also note that in this passage the term "a thousand years" is intended to convey the idea of "a very long time"; essentially a reign "without end", even though the term "a thousand years" is used, it is not meant to limit the duration but to suggest the vastness of it. See also numerous Biblical references to God owning the cattle on a thousand hills, or God's mercy being shown to a thousand generations. These phrases are not intended to limit God's providence or restrain His mercy to merely a thousand literal years, but to suggest that God's mercy and providence are essentially greater than we can hope for.)

Now, we do see a reference to the fact that "the rest of the dead did not come to life until the thousand years were completed." So, let's keep in mind who "the rest of the dead" are: those who did take the mark and who did worship the image of Nero. These are those who either actively participated in the persecution of Christians, or who passively gave their assent to it.

Either way, the ones who do not experience resurrection in this life (being made alive with Christ spiritually) will not experience resurrection in the next life until the final judgment, as we shall explore in greater detail later.

Note: The oldest complete manuscript of the scriptures—Codex Sinaiticus from the fourth century—does not contain the sentence that reads "The rest of the dead did not come to life until the thousand years were ended." Why not? Perhaps this sentence was added later by a scribe to attempt to clarify some confusion and it later ended up being incorporated into the text as if John himself had written it). At any rate, we may want to hold that particular verse a little loosely as we look to understand what John wanted to communicate about the resurrection.

WHAT IS THE RESURRECTION?

For some, the Resurrection is a literal event where the physical bodies of dead people will one day rise again and come out of the grave when Jesus returns. However, as we've seen, almost everything we know about Apocalyptic literature is that it describes spiritual realities and isn't meant to be taken literally. Why would we suppose that this one event where dead bodies come back to life is literal when every other reference we find is spiritual? Perhaps it's wise to at least consider the possibility that all of what we read in these passages is to be taken spiritually based on the established pattern.

So, is the resurrection a literal event where dead bodies will return to physical form again? Well, if we take a closer look we'll see that Jesus corrected the misconception that the resurrection would be a literal, physical reality when he told the Sadducees:

"For in the *resurrection* they neither marry nor are given in marriage, but are *like angels in heaven*." (Matt. 22:30)

So, the resurrection, according to Jesus, is something that takes places spiritually, not literally.

Jesus continues to make his point in the very next verse:

"But *regarding the resurrection of the dead*, have you not read what was spoken to you by God: 'I am the God of Abraham, and the God of Isaac, and the God of Jacob'? *He is not the God of the dead but of the living*." (Matt. 22:31) [emphasis mine]

Jesus here reminds us that God is now the God of those who have passed away long ago. How can this be unless, as Jesus argues, those who have died are not actually dead but are alive now in the spiritual sense? But that's not all Jesus has to say about the resurrection. Notice how he totally redefines the resurrection here:

> "Jesus said unto her, *I am the resurrection*, and the life: *he that believeth in me, though he were dead, yet shall he live.*" (John 11:25) [emphasis mine]

I'm not sure we really grasp the magnitude of this statement. Here, Jesus says that he is the resurrection. It's not an event out there in the future. It's a reality that is found in Christ. Also notice that Jesus says that it is those who are dead who will live this resurrection life that is only found in him. The one who believes has died. That fact doesn't change. What is significant is that the dead in this physical world are now alive through Christ in the spiritual world. This is the resurrection.

So, when Paul speaks of our resurrection in Christ as having already taken place, and in fact as something we currently experience, it should not come as much of a surprise to us:

> "*But God,* being rich in mercy, because of His great love with which He loved us, *even when we were dead in our transgressions, made us alive together with Christ (by grace you have been saved), and raised us up with Him,* and seated us with Him in the heavenly places in Christ Jesus, so that in the ages to come He might show the surpassing riches of His grace in kindness toward us in Christ Jesus." (Eph. 2:4–7) [emphasis mine]

When we were dead, in a spiritual sense, we were resurrected (spiritually) with Christ. And when we do eventually die, we will continue to experience life in Christ. This is our second resurrection.

Paul makes this same argument in 1 Corinthians 15 when he says:

> "It is sown a natural body; *it is raised a spiritual body.*" (1 Cor. 15:44)

The Body of Christ (the Church) is the spiritual body that has been raised. You and I are that spiritual body. So, we don't have to wait for some future day of transformation. Why? Because we have been "...fashioned like unto his glorious body, according to the working whereby he is able even to subdue all things unto himself." (Phil. 3:21)

This, again, is why Jesus can say:

> "Truly, truly, I say to you, *an hour is coming and now is,* when *the dead will hear the voice* of the Son of God, and *those who hear will live.*" (John 5:25) [emphasis mine]

Jesus is speaking in the context of the resurrection in this passage. He tells us that the hour is not only "coming" in the future, he also says the hour "now is" when "the dead" (in a spiritual sense) will hear his voice and "those who hear will live" in a spiritual sense. This is the mystery of the resurrection. People who are physically alive are spiritually dead. They experience resurrection life when they respond to the words of Jesus, even though they are physically alive. And those who are physically dead experience resurrection life after they die in a spiritual sense, not in a physical one. We therefore experience resurrection life now, and after we die. Even if we die without experiencing the first resurrection (in this life), we all experience the resurrection life after we physically die, as we see here when Jesus says:

> "Do not marvel at this; for an hour is coming, in which all who are in the tombs will hear His voice, and will come forth; *those who did the good deeds to a resurrection of life, those who committed the evil deeds to a resurrection of judgment.*" (John 5:28-29) [emphasis mine]

And when does this resurrection judgment take place? After we die:

> "For it is appointed for a man *once to die, and then the judgment.*" (Heb. 9:27-28) [emphasis mine]

So, the resurrection that Jesus speaks about is something that does not involve physical bodies coming to life again, but is all about spiritual souls being resurrected to life after they die. Paul affirms this idea and also tells us that we have already been raised (resurrected) with Christ because we were spiritually dead and now we are spiritually made alive again in Christ. This life will continue beyond the grave and at that time we will experience the second resurrection which will involve the judgment where both the righteous and the unrighteous will be purified in the presence of Christ for the purpose of restoring all things and making all things new, as promised.

SO, THE RESURRECTION THAT JESUS SPEAKS ABOUT IS SOMETHING THAT DOES NOT INVOLVE PHYSICAL BODIES COMING TO LIFE AGAIN, BUT IS ALL ABOUT SPIRITUAL SOULS BEING RESURRECTED TO LIFE AFTER THEY DIE.

As one Bible teacher, Brian Johnson phrased it:

> "Once we see… our ultimate destiny as fulfilled, or realize this eternal reality, then from the perspective of the consummation, or from the divine viewpoint of eternity, we can understand that we always were raised up into heavenly places, and always were partakers of his glorious body, the pre-existent or eternal body of the Christ. We are [chosen] in him before the foundation of the world. (Eph. 1:4) We sometimes come to this realization of eternal oneness step by step, little by little, and revelation by revelation. It is a new divine perspective. This realization is more than [Fulfillment] theology. However sometimes, it is through such a fulfilled eschatology that this divine viewpoint may open up to us."[3]

We were dead already, in a spiritual sense, and we were resurrected (also spiritually) with Christ. This means that there is no other resurrection to look forward to, nor is there any need for another one. We have the experience of spiritual resurrection now, in this life, and we have the future resurrection to spiritual life after we die. What more is there?

OUR DECISION TO MAKE

Now, there is one final verse in the Bible we need to answer before we move on. This one requires a bit more explanation:

> "But avoid worldly and empty chatter, for it will lead to further ungodliness, and their talk will spread like gangrene. Among them are Hymenaeus and Philetus, *men who have gone astray from the truth saying that the resurrection has already taken place,* and they upset the faith of some." (2 Tim. 2:16–18) [emphasis mine]

After everything we've seen so far, this verse appears to put the brakes on the entire thing. We've heard from Jesus and from the Apostle Paul that the resurrection is a spiritual reality, not a physical one. We've heard Jesus affirm that, in the resurrection we will be like the angels (spiritual, not physical), and that those who die will live because of Him. We've read the words of Paul who affirms that we who are alive now have already experienced the resurrection in this life and will experience it again after we die. We've also seen that the righteous and the unrighteous will be resurrected to face the judgment. And now, we have this one single verse that stands in our way and seems to throw a wrench in the entire argument. What do we do?

Well, I believe we have a choice to make. We either listen to the wealth of instruction we've received from both Jesus and the Apostle Paul on this topic and chose to ignore this passage in 2

Timothy, or we choose to disregard everything Jesus and Paul have to say in these passages above and base our entire belief of the resurrection on this one solitary verse. Which is it?

To be honest, I want you to make up your own mind. Everyone needs to decide for themselves which to accept and which to reject. However, I would suggest that you consider a few things about the epistle of 2 Timothy before you make your decision. For example, many New Testament scholars agree that the Apostle Paul did not write this letter of 2 Timothy. In fact, the "Pastoral Epistles" are the most disputed of all of those attributed to Paul. There are several reasons for doubting Pauline authorship of 2 Timothy and the other "Pastorals." For example:

- The vocabulary and phraseology used is often at variance with that of the undisputed epistles.

- Over a third of the vocabulary is not used anywhere else in the Pauline epistles.

- Over one-fifth of the vocabulary is not used anywhere else in the entire New Testament.

- Two-thirds of the vocabulary in 2 Timothy was of the type commonly used by Second Century Christian writers, not First Century.

- Paul's travels to Crete (Titus 1:5–6), again to Ephesus (1 Tim 1:3), Nicopolis (Titus 3:12), and Troas (2 Tim 1:15, 4:13) cannot be fit into any reconstruction of Paul's life or works as determined from the undisputed epistles or from Acts.

- Historians like Bart Ehrman suggest that Second Century proto-orthodox Christians had motivation to forge the

Pastorals to combat the Gnostic use of other Pauline epistles.

- The Pastoral Epistles describe the character and requirements for bishops, elders and deacons which many scholars agree were offices which did not appear during Paul's lifetime.

- The theology contained in these epistles is more reflective of Second Century than First Century Christian thought.

- Specifically, the Second Century Christians (post AD 70) had begun to reevaluate the meaning of the Second Coming of Christ as being far away, whereas the First Century Christians understood it as being near, (pre AD 70).

- The Pastoral Epistles condemn forms of Hellenic mysticism and gnosticism which were quite insignificant in the First Century.

So, we're left, as I said, with a choice. We can balance everything we believe about the Resurrection on this one verse in 2 Timothy—which may, or may not, have been written by the Apostle Paul—*or* we can base our belief on the vast number of verses from Jesus and the Gospels and the undisputed epistles of Paul that we've looked at so far.

Again, I will let you decide for yourself. As the authentic Apostle Paul encouraged us, "Let everyone be convinced in their own minds." (Rom. 14:5) I believe I have already made up my own mind on this subject.

For now, let's assume that what Jesus and the Apostle have to say on this subject is accurate: The resurrection is Christ. We can experience it right now while we are still living, in a purely spiritual sense, and we will experience a second resurrection when we eventually die and come alive again in Christ—also in a purely spiritual sense.

Since everything else we read in the Apocalyptic literature of the Bible is spiritual, and not literal, there's little reason (in my opinion) to assume that the resurrection passages are descriptions of literal dead bodies coming back to physical life again.

Your mileage may vary.

CHAPTER 10

THE FUTURE IS NOW

"The mind that opens up to a new idea never returns to its original size."

— ALBERT EINSTEIN

So, where does all of this leave us? If every End Times prophecy in the Bible is already fulfilled in Christ and the events of 70 AD, what does that mean for us today? Is there anything to look forward to? Are we just supposed to meander through life and wait to die? Hardly.

The question: *"What do we have to look forward to?"* tends to ignore all that has already gone before us. We live in the age of fulfillment. God has accomplished His grand plan. *"It is finished!"* was the victory cry of Christ. The prophecy concerning the coming of the Messiah, the end of the Old Covenant, the establishment of a New Covenant, the dwelling of God among us, the Holy Spirit poured out on all flesh, the promised end of the age, the destruction of the physical temple, the establishment of the future End Times temple (the Church), the new priesthood of all believers, the new Incarnation of Christ in each and every one of us and the promised reality of resurrection life today, and after we die are all now gloriously and fantastically fulfilled. These are the days that the angels longed to look into and the Old Testament prophets longed to see. For us they are here and now realities. And our only response is: "What's next?"

This is like that old Janet Jackson song, "What Have You Done For Me Lately?" where all that matters is whatever new experience we can look forward to next rather than stopping to take stock of—and fully appreciate—all the vast treasures of God's exceptional goodness we are wallowing in right now. Not that we don't continue to experience God's goodness on a daily basis, of course. But we should do so without taking all that God has already done for granted.

> **WE'VE BEEN TRAINED TO TURN TO OUR BIBLES FOR SOME FUTURE HOPE. WE NEED SOME DISTANT GOAL POST TO LOOK TOWARDS. WE ARE HARD-WIRED TO RACE FOR THE FINISH LINE SOMEWHERE OUT THERE BEYOND THE HORIZON.**

Still, I get it. We've been trained to turn to our Bibles for some future hope. We need some distant goal post to look towards. We are hard-wired to race for the finish line somewhere out there beyond the horizon.

"*What do we have to look forward to?*" you may ask. Well, first of all, let's understand that all of these fulfilled prophecies in our past create glorious possibilities for us in our present day reality. As Arthur J. Melanson reminds us:

> "Some of the things Jesus did were one-time events. The cross was a one-time event, but sinners still look to Calvary for their atonement. The Second Coming [in AD 70] was a one-time event, but all Christians continue to reap the benefits of the kingdom of God that shall never pass away... So some things are one-time events but have enduring qualities. Other things are not one-time events but only began in the first century and continue today and forever. Judgment is one, and resurrection is another."[1]

So, rather than place our hope in a future event that Christians have been anticipating and sitting around waiting for the last few hundred years or more, why don't we take heart in knowing that Jesus has already returned, and has empowered us to continually advance His Kingdom and share His Gospel message of hope to our world?

The good news is that we are no longer paralyzed as we wait for Jesus to come and fix things. We now understand that His plan all along was for us to sow this Kingdom like seed, and to act as yeast that spreads throughout the entire lump, and to become agents of transformation who slowly, but surely, bring the kingdoms of this world to ruin and establish His Kingdom forever.

The truth is this: *There is more of Christ in the world right now than there was when Jesus walked the earth almost two-thousand years ago.* Don't believe me? It's true.

Jesus, who promised never to leave us or forsake us, poured out his Spirit on all flesh—men and women, young and old, Jew and Gentile. This is only the beginning. He went away because it was better for us in every way. We didn't understand it before, but now we do. And so we eagerly step forward and take our place at the forefront of this Heavenly strategy that is already at work in our world—and in every one of us!

We have been deputized by the Holy Spirit. We are filled with the fullness of the One who fills everything in every way. Our mission is to be the hands and feet of Christ to everyone around us. Why? Because we now understand that the "Second Coming" of Christ was fulfilled at Pentecost when the Spirit of the Living God was poured out "on all flesh" in fulfillment of the promise of a New Covenant whereby God would dwell among mankind by His Spirit and make a home within every single one of us.

Ever since, Jesus has been slowly returning—one person at a time—as Christ is revealed and awakened within yet another person made in the image of God.

As Christ abides in you and you abide in Christ, the presence of Christ is incarnated once more.

"By this, love is perfected with us...because as He is, so also are we in this world." (1 John 4:17)

An essential element of the Messianic promise is this: Nothing will ever be the same again. God makes this clear in Isaiah 65:17 when He says:

"See, I will create new heavens and a new earth. The former things will not be remembered, nor will they come to mind."

What follows is a long list of contrasts between the way things are, and the way things will be after the Messiah comes: If there was death, there will be life. If there was violence, there will be peace. If there was despair, there will be hope.

Simply put: Jesus changes everything. Best of all, the Messianic promise includes the renewal of humankind itself. So, not only will God make all things new, He will make all people new, as He says through Ezekiel:

"I will give you a new heart and put a new spirit in you; I will remove from you your heart of stone and give you a heart of flesh." (Ezekiel 36:26)

The reason why we are made new is so that we can contain the new life of Christ within, or as Jesus phrases it:

"People don't pour new wine into old wineskins. If they do, the skins will burst; the wine will run out and the wineskins will be ruined. No, they pour new wine into new wineskins, and both are preserved." (Matt. 9:17)

In other words, we need to be made new so we can receive the spirit of renewal within. We become agents of the new order;

carriers of the renewal; catalysts of the resurrection. This is why Paul says:

> "Therefore, if anyone is in Christ, the new creation has come: The old has gone, the new is here!" (2 Cor. 5:17)

Honestly, I don't believe any of us can fully grasp the magnitude of this statement. The old creation has faded away. There is now, literally, a new heaven and a new earth and a new humanity unleashed upon us.

Elsewhere, Paul says that we who are in Christ are taking off the old self in order "to be made new in the attitude of your minds; and to put on the new self, created to be like God in true righteousness and holiness." (Eph. 4:23-24)

This is the entire plan: To remake the world from within, the way a small pinch of yeast spreads to transform the entire lump of dough and slowly begins to rise.

As John describes it in his Revelation of Jesus, when the Bride of Christ (that's us) unites with Jesus here on the Earth, everything begins to change. He and the Father come to make their home in us. Together, we experience the promise of the New Covenant where God's dwelling is now among us, and where He is our God, and we are His people. From this divine/human connection, God shouts "Behold! I am making everything new!" (Rev. 21:5)

This genetic transformation has already begun. We are the new wineskins that are filled with the new wine. We are the new generation of the resurrection of Christ. We are the New Jerusalem that has come down from God out of heaven. We are the New Temple of God where Christ lives today. We are the Body of Christ walking around in the world today. We are children of God that all creation eagerly anticipates. (See Romans 8:19)

SLOWLY, INEVITABLY, IRREVERSIBLY, CHRIST IS COMING—AND WILL CONTINUE TO COME INTO THIS WORLD—ONE LIFE, ONE INCARNATION AT A TIME, UNTIL EVENTUALLY EVERY KNEE WILL BOW AND EVERY TONGUE WILL GLADLY CONFESS THAT CHRIST IS INDEED THE LORD OF ALL, TO THE GLORY OF GOD OUR FATHER.

Because Jesus, our Messiah, has come, nothing—and no one—will ever be the same again. As more and more people realize Christ is alive and breathing within them, Christ's Kingdom expands, Christ's voice is heard, Christ's heart beats louder, Christ's hands reach out, Christ's love is expressed, and received, and felt in the heart of yet another person where Christ is soon to be resurrected and revived within.

"All of creation eagerly awaits the moment when the sons of God are revealed." (Romans 8:19)

Slowly, inevitably, irreversibly, Christ is coming—and will continue to come into this world—one life, one incarnation at a time, until eventually every knee will bow and every tongue will gladly confess that Christ is indeed the Lord of all, to the glory of God our Father.

The Spirit and the Bride say: "Come, Lord!"

And Jesus says, "I will never leave you, nor forsake you."

"Even so," the Church cries out, "Come quickly, Lord Jesus!"

Jesus replies: "Abide in me, and I will abide in you."

Look around you. Look within. There is more of Christ in the world today than there was 2,000 years ago.

This slow-motion second coming is ongoing, irresistible, and almost nearly imperceptibly a relentless wave of love crashing even now against the shores of humanity.

Wake up. The Kingdom of God is here.

Rejoice.

Now, go and be the Incarnation of Christ in your community. Join with millions of other Christ-filled Incarnations who also work daily to transform their world into the Kingdom of God.

Jesus has returned. He is alive within you. Living and breathing inside your skin. You are His hands. You are His feet. You are what all creation has been groaning for. Not later. Now. Not one day. Today. What is the hope of glory? It is Christ in you!

Take courage. In this world you will have trouble. But Christ has overcome this world. You are not alone. Emmanuel—literally God with us—is abiding within you and has promised never to leave you or to forsake you. Nothing will ever separate you from Him or His love for you. This means you can experience the presence of Christ within you becoming more and more real with every passing moment until one day you see Him face to face. Until then, you and Christ are cosmically, and spiritually intertwined into one—this same great mystery that Paul attempted to describe when he spoke of a man and woman becoming "one" and yet reminded us that he was speaking of Christ and His Bride—that's you and me—inexplicably interwoven together for all eternity.

The kingdoms of this world will one day be replaced by the Kingdom of our God. This is inevitable. You and I get to actively participate in this unprecedented transformation process where God literally "makes all things new" and even though this process started 2,000 years ago, for you and me it starts right now.

So, what do you have to look forward to? More than you can possibly imagine.

But whatever you do, don't wait. Don't postpone this process. The Kingdom of God is already advancing. Everything is set into motion.

Trust me; you wouldn't want to get left behind.

A WORD OF HOPE

After the prompting of my friend, Brad Jersak, I've realized the need to provide a final word of hope to the book before closing this out.

As he noted to me, there are some reading this who might find my vision of a world without a literal Second Coming of Christ to be a little less than thrilling. Specifically, for those who have lost loved ones, or who are suffering in this life—whether through sickness, or poverty, or cultural oppression—the absence of a future hope of heaven is anything but Good News and might even seem bleak, dark and empty for many.

So, let me take this last chapter to assure you of a few things. First, that it is my sincere hope for everyone that, when we die, we all enter into the presence of Christ. This is a universal hope for all mankind, not just for Christians.

As I demonstrated in my previous book, *Jesus Undefeated*, the early Christians largely embraced this view of Universal Reconciliation, or Ultimate Reconciliation. In this view, everyone who dies will face the Judgment which was metaphorically described as "passing through the fire." This "fire" symbolized the spiritual purification process by which the light of Christ is revealed in us and everyone is made new again in His presence.

I believe this is the ultimate reality that we will all experience when we breathe our last breath in this life and awaken in the next one.

I would also like to affirm that this awakening in the presence of Christ after we die is what the scriptures refer to as the "Second Resurrection" where we are all raised to life again into an imperishable existence where God wipes every tear from our eyes and we reign and abide with Christ forever.

Finally, I would argue that this new reality we find ourselves in after we die, and where we all experience this Second Resurrection and undergo this spiritual purification process is what we might describe as the future Kingdom of Christ on earth. How is this possible? Because I do believe that the plan that Jesus has set into motion almost 2,000 years ago will eventually and inevitably overwhelm the entire planet and transform each and every person into the glorious likeness of Christ. This process is already underway. We can see the effects of Christ's Kingdom all through history up to this point, and we can experience this reality of transformation in our own lives today.

THIS PROCESS IS ALREADY UNDERWAY. WE CAN SEE THE EFFECTS OF CHRIST'S KINGDOM ALL THROUGH HISTORY UP TO THIS POINT, AND WE CAN EXPERIENCE THIS REALITY OF TRANSFORMATION IN OUR OWN LIVES TODAY.

One day, without fail, all of humanity will eventually awaken to the beauty and simplicity of Christ's teachings. One day everyone will know God intimately. One day everyone will agree that it is better to love our enemies than to kill them. One day every single person on earth will become persuaded to beat their swords into plowshares and resolve to study war no longer. One day—and it might take a very long time—the kingdoms of this world will become transformed into the Kingdom of Christ. One day the yeast will indeed spread throughout the entire lump of dough and the mustard seed will sprout and grow into a massive tree that covers the entire planet.

This is the world we will awaken in, I believe, whenever our bodies expire, and we experience death. This world will be in the making while we sleep, but as far as we experience it the transition will be nearly instantaneous. We will close our eyes here and open them in Christ's eternal Kingdom which will one day be established forever when God, at last, makes all things perfectly, wondrously new.

So, if you're hoping for a future reality where you are reunited with your loved ones, and where there is no longer any pain or death; where we are all healed and restored in the presence of Jesus and we see him face-to-face, then I have some good news for you: This is what I think all of creation is destined for.

We are in the presence of Christ now. We are tethered to Christ by an unbreakable love that nothing—not even death—can sever. We are alive in Christ today, and we will be alive in Christ for all eternity to come.

God is love. His love endures forever. We are created in the image of God, who is love, and this means we are also destined to endure forever in the heart of the One who loves us beyond measure, and without end.

I'll see you there soon.

FOR FURTHER READING

- *Before Jerusalem Fell* by Ken Gentry

- *The Ephesians Road Out Of Dispensationalism* by Ken Gentry

- *Revelation: Four Views* by Steve Gregg

- *How The End Times Ended In 70 A.D.* by Micah J. Stephens

- *Josephus: Complete Works*, translated by William Whiston

- *Sinners In The Hands Of A Loving God* by Brian Zahnd

WAS REVELATION WRITTEN PRIOR TO 70 AD?

This article will attempt to address that question and make a case for the earlier date, previous to the destruction of Jerusalem in AD 70, as opposed to the later date under the Emperor Domitian.

Why does this matter? Because if Revelation is about the coming destruction of Jerusalem in AD 70, then the case can be made (as I have done) that the letter was written to warn First Century Christians of that event and to identify The Beast (Nero) and to provide prophetic context for what was soon to take place.

If, however, if it can be shown that John wrote Revelation *after* the fall of Jerusalem, then it must be something else; either it was a letter written to explain to those Christians who had just witnessed the distressing events of 70 AD as a way to help them make sense of everything from a prophetic perspective, or it was potentially written as a warning to Christians in future days about events that have not yet happened.

Personally, I find it very hard to believe that any early Christians who lived through the events of 70 AD would respond by sitting down to write a long apocalyptic epistle without once mentioning or referring to such a cataclysmic event, at least in passing. However, I have many other (better) reasons for doubting the late dating of this book of Revelation, as we shall see.

THE OPPOSITION

Before I share my reasons for claiming the earlier date, let's examine why some believe it was written after the reign of Nero. First, because there is conflicting testimony concerning when John was exiled to the island of Patmos (where he wrote the epistle). Some have said that he was exiled there by Domitian (who came after Nero) and was on the island between 81 AD and 96 AD. However, there are also many historical documents that contradict that claim and say that John was exiled during the reign of Nero (before AD 70).

The strongest evidence for a later date comes from Irenaeus (120-202 AD) who claimed that John wrote his Revelation under the reign of Domitian. However, Irenaeus had a pretty lousy track record for historical accuracy. For example, he also wrote that Jesus' ministry lasted twenty years and that he was crucified at age 50. No one takes those claims seriously, so perhaps we shouldn't take his word for the date of John's Revelation either.

Here are 10 reasons why I believe we can confidently accept the early date of Revelation rather than the later date.

REASON 1: JOHN IDENTIFIES NERO AS THE CURRENT EMPEROR

In Revelation 17:10 John says this: "They are also seven kings. Five have fallen, one is, the other has not yet come; but when he does come, he must remain for only a little while"

Here, John is attempting to identify the meaning of the 7 headed beast. He says that the seven heads are seven kings and then says that the previous five have died, and the sixth one is still living. If we start with Julius Caesar (the first Emperor of Rome) and start counting, we'll find that the sixth Caesar—the one who is now ruling—is Nero.

Could it be any clearer than that? John himself tells us that the ruler of the Roman Empire at the time he is writing his epistle is the sixth Caesar and that was none other than Nero. (See previous chapters in this book regarding the identity of the Beast and the meaning of the "Mark of the Beast".)

> COULD IT BE ANY CLEARER THAN THAT? JOHN HIMSELF TELLS US THAT THE RULER OF THE ROMAN EMPIRE AT THE TIME HE IS WRITING HIS EPISTLE IS THE SIXTH CAESAR AND THAT WAS NONE OTHER THAN NERO.

REASON 2: THE SYRIAC NEW TESTAMENT

One of the oldest known New Testament documents is from the second century and it is called The Syriac, or the Peshitto. In this early version if you turn to the Book of Revelation you'll see this on the title page:

> "Again the revelation which was upon the holy John the Evangelist from God when he was on the island of Patmos where he was thrown by the emperor Nero."

Since Nero ruled Rome from AD 54 to AD 68, John had to have written his epistle during this time period.

REASON 3: JEWISH PERSECUTION OF CHRISTIANS.

The New Testament reveals that, almost from the beginning, the Jewish rulers persecuted the early church. Paul, the Apostle, was himself a member of the group that went around arresting and harassing those who followed Jesus as Messiah. This persecution by Jews continued and intensified until something drastic happened: The Jewish Temple was destroyed, Jerusalem was ravaged and the Jewish system of religion was effectively dismantled.

Because John refers to Jewish persecution in Revelation as something that Christians were still enduring at the time of his writing, this means that the Temple was still standing and therefore we can date his Revelation as being written before AD 70.

REASON 4: JUDAIZERS WITHIN THE CHURCH

According to John's epistle, Judaizers were very active at the time of his writing.

> "'I know your tribulation and your poverty (but you are rich), and the blasphemy by those who say they are Jews and are not, but are a synagogue of Satan." (Rev. 2:9)

> "Behold, I will cause those of the synagogue of Satan, who say that they are Jews and are not, but lie—I will make them come and bow down at your feet, and make them know that I have loved you." (Rev. 3:9)

This would have not been any issue if the Jerusalem Temple had been destroyed when John wrote his letter.

In addition, once Paul's letters against Judaizers (Galatians, Romans, and Ephesians) were published and circulated throughout the early church (something that we can assume came after John's Revelation letter), this activity would not have been so easily tolerated.

So, after Paul's letters denouncing Judaizers this would not have been an issue. The fact that John addresses the issue means that Paul's letters had not yet been written and circulated. Therefore, Revelation was written before Galatians, Romans and Ephesians, which means it was Pre-AD 70.

REASON 5: THE EXISTENCE OF JERUSALEM AND THE TEMPLE

In Revelation, Chapter 11, John is told to go and to "measure the temple of God and the altar, and those who worship in it." (v. 1)

If the Temple had been destroyed, John could not have done this. Therefore, John's Revelation was probably written before the destruction of Jerusalem in AD 70.

REASON 6: EVENTS TO COME "SHORTLY" AND "SOON"

All throughout Revelation, John continues to remind his readers that the events he is foreshadowing in his letter will come to pass "shortly" or "soon" or "quickly". If he meant that these events would happen more than 2,000 years later, he certainly could have said so. But he didn't.

> "The Revelation of Jesus Christ, which God gave Him to show to His bond-servants, the things which must soon take place…" (Rev. 1:1)

> "Blessed is he who reads and those who hear the words of the prophecy, and heed the things which are written in it; for the time is near. " (Rev. 1:3)

> "And he said to me, "Do not seal up the words of the prophecy of this book, for the time is near." (Rev. 22:10)

> "He who testifies to these things says, "Yes, I am coming quickly." Amen. Come, Lord Jesus." (Rev. 22:20)

REASON 7: CHRIST SEEN BY "THOSE WHO PIERCED HIM"

To explain this reason (and the reference above from Rev. 22:20) it's necessary to first explain what we mean by the "Coming" of

Jesus, as opposed to the "Return of Christ" at the End of the World.

There are several references throughout the entire Bible to judgment events as "the coming of God". For example, in the OT we find prophecies about God's judgment against certain nations expressed this way:

> "Behold, the LORD rideth upon a swift cloud, and shall come into Egypt: and the idols of Egypt shall be moved at his presence, and the heart of Egypt shall melt in the midst of it." (Isaiah 19:1)

Did God actually ride on a cloud and attack Egypt? No. But the Assyrian army did attack Egypt in fulfillment of this prophecy around the 7th century BC.

It's in the same way that Jesus says that he will "come in the clouds" to bring judgment against Jerusalem for rejecting him and his gospel. For example, Jesus tells the High Priest that he will personally see Jesus coming on the clouds with power:

> "Jesus said to him, "You have said it yourself; nevertheless I tell you, hereafter you will see the Son of Man sitting at the right hand of Power, and coming on the clouds of heaven." (Matthew 26:64)

This was a promise made to a certain man, Caiphas, the High Priest: "You will see the Son of Man…coming on the clouds of heaven."

Jesus also prophesied during his Olivet Discourse, (which is all about the destruction of the temple), the following:

> "And then the sign of the Son of Man will appear in the sky, and then all the tribes of the earth will mourn, and they will see the Son of Man coming on the clouds of the sky with power and great glory." (Matt. 24:30)

So, having said all of that, let's look at what John says in Revelation:

"Behold, he is coming with the clouds, and every eye will see Him, even those who pierced Him; and all the tribes of the earth will mourn over Him. So it is to be. Amen." (Revelation 1:7) [emphasis mine]

Here, John says that the same people who crucified Christ will see him "coming in the clouds" which not only aligns with Jesus' own words, but also points to a coming Judgment against Jerusalem by using the phrase "coming in the clouds" as a reference to those OT passages above.

Just for the record, "those who pierced him" were not alive in AD 96 when some believe John wrote Revelation. How do we know this? Because they were all killed in AD 70 when the Romans destroyed Jerusalem. Therefore, "those who pierced him" were still alive before AD 70 and that means John had to have written his letter when they were still living.

REASON 8: JOHN'S CONDITION IN AD 96

We know from the writings of Jerome (an early Church Father), that John the Apostle was seen in AD 96 and that he was quite frail, saying:

"…he was with difficulty carried to the church, and could speak only a few words to the people."

However, if we read Revelation 10:11 John says:

"[I must] prophesy again concerning many peoples and nations and tongues and kings."

If John wrote Revelation in AD 96, when we have an eyewitness who says he was barely able to walk or speak at that time, then how could John continue to speak to anyone in that condition?

However, if John wrote Revelation in AD 70, he had many years of life left to speak to many nations and kings about the Gospel of Jesus before AD 96.

REASON 9: DANIEL'S PROPHECY

When the prophet Daniel was given his prophecy by the angel of God, he is told to "seal up the vision, for it is a long way off" (See Daniel 12:4). But the things he wrote about were only about 483 years away. Yet John is told "not to seal up the vision". Why? Because he is told his prophecy "concerns things which must shortly come to pass" (See Rev. 22:10).

If the events in John's prophecy were just a few years away (10 or 20 years' time), then all of this would make sense. However, if Daniel's prophecy was sealed because it was "a long way off" (483 years), it makes no sense that John's prophecy was *not* sealed if it "must shortly come to pass" more than 2,000 years later?!

For this reason, I believe that John's Revelation was written before the destruction of Jerusalem in AD 70.

REASON 10: ONLY SEVEN CHURCHES?

John's letter begins with a series of specific messages given by Jesus to the Seven Churches in Asia Minor. If John's epistle were written after AD 70, say in AD 96 as some suggest, there would have been many, many more churches in that region than just seven.

IN CONCLUSION

These, I believe, are the ten best reasons for accepting the early date for the writing of John's Revelation and for interpreting the events found in this epistle as being fulfilled by the destruction of Jerusalem by the Romans in AD 70.[1]

THE BLOOD MOON HOAX EXPOSED

No doubt you've heard of the Blood Moon prophecies that many are saying point to the imminent return of Christ, or "something big about to happen" in the Middle East.

If not, here's a quick overview: A Blood Moon is simply a lunar eclipse where the moon appears red in color due to the sunlight passing through Earth's atmosphere and casting a red shadow on the moon's surface. The significance that many Christians are getting excited about lately is that the Jewish Feasts of Passover and Tabernacles in 2014 and 2015 will coincide with a total of four Blood Moons. Some want us to see these lunar events as signs that God is doing something new, or about to shake things up in the Middle East.

Of course, these same people also want us to buy their book on the subject. People like John Hagee and Mark Blitz, for example. But let's examine their arguments and see if there's anything to this hype.

First of all, the argument in favor of the legitimacy of these Blood Moon signs hinges on the supposition that previous Blood Moon events have proven to be signs of historic significance.

For example, they claim that there were four blood moons at Passover and the Feast of Tabernacles in 1492 which coincided with the expulsion of Jews from Spain and the discovery of the Americas by Columbus. Then they say that there were four blood moons in 1948 which was a sign of the Israeli War of Independence, and that the four blood moons in 1967 was a sign of Israel's military action to repossess the Old City of Jerusalem.

Sound convincing? Well…not exactly. First of all, the Jewish calendar is a lunar calendar. That means that their feasts and festivals always coincide with full moon events. It also means that lunar eclipses—which only occur when the moon is full—are not rare events in Jewish history. We'll examine this in more detail later, but first let's examine those historic events in light of actual evidence.

The lunar eclipse in 1492 wasn't a "sign" of the expulsion of Jews from Spain. Why? Because the Tribunal that expelled them was established November 1, 1478 which occurred 15 years before the lunar eclipse. Hardly a sign or a warning is it? Plus, the Alhambra Decree, which officially ordered of expulsion of Jews from Spain, was issued in January 1492, which was about 15 months before the lunar eclipse referenced.

The 1948 eclipse is also not a sign of the Israeli war of independence. Why? Because that war began on May 15, 1948 and ended March 10, 1949. The first of the four lunar eclipses didn't happen until just over a month after the war ended. Why would God give anyone a sign about something that had already taken place? That, by definition, is not a sign from God.

The 1967 eclipse is not a sign of Israeli forces taking possession of the Old City of Jerusalem. Why not? Because that took place on June 7, 1967 and the lunar eclipse took place 44 days before that, and—most importantly—it was not visible from Jerusalem. The next set of blood moons occurred over the following year and a half, and so again was after the fact.

So, in what way are any of these events "signs" of anything? It's like someone shouting "Look out for that car!" an hour after your car accident. Most of these blood moon "signs" are not visible from Jerusalem, and/or occur long after the events have already taken place.

Let's be clear, nothing can truly be considered "a sign from God" unless a prophet of God speaks a prophecy—in advance of the event—and then the sign is given as a proof.

Keep in mind: No prophecy preceded any of these events and no one gave these lunar eclipses and signs in advance as proofs. No one predicted that the Jews would be expelled from Spain before it happened, for example. So just because things happen we can't run around looking for signs after the fact. It doesn't work that way.

Here's another point: Tetrads (or the occurrence of four consecutive lunar eclipses) are very common. They are not rare. They happen very, very often, in fact. Over the last 4,000 years there have been numerous lunar tetrads (or Blood Moons) on record and between 1999 BC and today there have been 111 Blood Moons.

MOST OF THESE BLOOD MOON "SIGNS" ARE NOT VISIBLE FROM JERUSALEM, AND/OR OCCUR LONG AFTER THE EVENTS HAVE ALREADY TAKEN PLACE.

Do you know what significant events coincided with all of those? None. Because they happen all the time and are therefore not "signs" of anything happening in the world. It would be like pointing to the migration of Canada Geese as a sign of some political shift in China. The two events are not related, and one of those events (the migration of Canada Geese) happens every year about the same time, regardless of what's happening in Chinese politics.

Of the 55 Blood Moons that have occurred since the First Century AD, there have been 7 which coincided with Jewish Holy Days, and none of them were seen as signs of anything significant at the time.

To put everything in another perspective, here are some very significant events in the history of the nation of Israel which *did not* coincide with any Blood Moon signs.

There were no Blood Moons during:

- 1446 BC (Israel left Egypt in the Exodus)

- 1406 BC (Joshua entered Canaan)

- 723 BC (Ten northern tribes went into Assyrian Captivity)

- 587 BC (Judah went into Babylonian captivity)

- 538 BC (Cyrus proclaims the Jews could return to Canaan)

- 533 BC (Jews began return from Babylon and arrived in Jerusalem)

- 1-2 BC (Jesus was born)

- 33 AD (Jesus was crucified) *Solar, but not lunar eclipse

- 70 AD (Jerusalem and the Temple destroyed by Romans)

- 135 AD (Hadrian renamed the city of Jerusalem, killed many Jews and expelled the rest)

- 1943 AD (Hitler killed 6 million Jews during the Holocaust)

Put another way, here are four more examples of when Tetrads (or a series of four Blood Moons) fell on all four Jewish feast days:

- 162 AD

- 795 AD

- 842 AD

- 860 AD

Guess what significant historic events happened during these Blood Moons? Wrong. Nothing happened. This is why authors like Hagee and Blitz totally ignore these, because they can't point to anything that seems to support their bogus theory.

THE LUNAR CALENDAR

Statistically, speaking, since Passover and the Feast of Tabernacles always happen on full moons, and take place on the 15th day of two different months within the year, there is a 1-in-6 chance that an eclipse will occur in at least one of these festivals annually.

In the twentieth century, 37 of the 230 lunar eclipses fell on either Passover or the Feast of Tabernacles, which is mildly fascinating, but completely irrelevant to anyone interested in Biblical prophecy.

So, in conclusion, don't waste your time—or your money—on anything related to this Blood Moon hoax. It's designed to stir up fear, and loosen your wallet. Nothing more.

Now, what if something significant *does* happen between now and the end of these four Blood Moon signs that is still forthcoming? Well, things happen all the time. My point is that if anything does happen in the world, we cannot point to the Blood Moons as any sort of prophetic sign.

Enjoy the lunar eclipse. Take good pictures. Marvel at God's creation. But don't give in to the fear and the hype. The Blood

Moons are not signs of anything other than the Glory of God as the Heavens declare His majesty and pour fourth speech all day long.

Note: This article was informed from a variety of sources, including the blog of Steve Rudd[1] and the blog of Richard Edmondson.[2]

101 SCRIPTURE REFERENCES TO CHALLENGE FUTURISM

The Dispensational Futurists view of the End Times hinges on the false assumption that the prophetic events found in the Scriptures are still yet to be fulfilled. However, the Scriptures themselves quickly refute this claim.

Here are over 100 verses that speak of the fulfillment coming "soon" or that the "time is near" or that the time is "at hand"; all of which provide the proof necessary to silence the Futurist position.

1. "The Kingdom of Heaven is at hand." (Matt. 3:2)

2. "Who warned you to flee from the wrath about to come?" (Matt. 3:7)

3. "The axe is already laid at the root of the trees." (Matt. 3:10)

4. "His winnowing fork is in His hand." (Matt. 3:12)

5. "The kingdom of heaven is at hand." (Matt. 4:17)

6. "The kingdom of heaven is at hand." (Matt. 10:7)

7. "You shall not finish going through the cities of Israel, until the Son of Man comes." (Matt. 10:23)

8. "....the age about to come." (Matt. 12:32)

9. "The Son of Man is about to come in the glory of His Father with His angels; and will then recompense every man according to his deeds." (Matt. 16:27)

10. "There are some of those who are standing here who shall not taste death until they see the Son of Man coming in His kingdom." (Matt. 16:28; cf. Mk. 9:1; Lk. 9:27)

11. "'When the owner of the vineyard comes, what will he do to those vine-growers?'... 'He will bring those wretches to a wretched end, and will rent out the vineyard to other vine-growers, who will pay him the proceeds at the proper seasons.'... 'Therefore I say to you, the kingdom of God will be taken away from you, and be given to a nation producing the fruit of it.'... When the chief priests and the Pharisees heard His parables, they understood that He was speaking about them." (Matt. 21:40-41,43,45)

12. "This generation will not pass away until all these things take place." (Matt. 24:34)

13. "From now on, you [Caiaphas, the chief priests, the scribes, the elders, the whole Sanhedrin] shall be seeing the Son of Man sitting at the right hand of Power, and coming on the clouds of heaven." (Matt. 26:64; Mk. 14:62; Lk. 22:69)

14. "The kingdom of God is at hand." (Mk. 1:15)

15. "What will the owner of the vineyard do? He will come and destroy the vine-growers, and will give the vineyard to others... They [the chief priests, scribes and elders] understood that He spoke the parable against them." (Mk. 12:9,12)

16. "This generation will not pass away until all these things take place." (Mk. 13:30)

17. "Who warned you to flee from the wrath about to come?" (Lk. 3:7)

18. "The axe is already laid at the root of the trees..." (Lk. 3:9)

19. "His winnowing fork is in His hand..." (Lk. 3:17)

20. "The kingdom of God has come near to you." (Lk. 10:9)

21. "The kingdom of God has come near." (Lk. 10:11)

22. "What, therefore, will the owner of the vineyard do to them? He will come and destroy these vine-growers and will give the vineyard to others."... The scribes and the chief priests... understood that He spoke this parable against them." (Lk. 20:15-16,19)

23. "These are days of vengeance, in order that all things which are written may be fulfilled." (Lk. 21:22)

24. "This generation will not pass away until all things take place." (Lk. 21:32)

25. "Daughters of Jerusalem, stop weeping for Me, but weep for yourselves and for your children. For behold, the days are coming when they will say, 'Blessed are the

barren, and the wombs that never bore, and the breasts that never nursed.' Then they will begin to say to the mountains, 'Fall on us,' and to the hills, 'Cover us.'" (Lk. 23:28-30; compare Rev. 6:14-17)

26. "We were hoping that He was the One who is about to redeem Israel." (Lk. 24:21)

27. "'I will come to you... In that Day you shall know that I am in My Father, and you in Me, and I in you.'... 'Lord, what then has happened that You are about to disclose Yourself to us, and not to the world?'" (Jn. 14:18, 20, 22)

28. "If I want him to remain until I come, what is that to you?" (Jn. 21:22)

29. "This is what was spoken of through the prophet Joel: 'And it shall be in the last days...'" (Acts 2:16-17)

30. "He has fixed a day in which He is about to judge the world in righteousness..." (Acts 17:31)

31. "There is about to be a resurrection of both the righteous and the wicked." (Acts 24:15)

32. "As he was discussing righteousness, self-control and the judgment about to come..." (Acts 24:25)

33. "Not for [Abraham's] sake only was it written, that [faith] was reckoned to him [as righteousness], but for our sake also, to whom it is about to be reckoned." (Rom. 4:23-24)

34. "If you are living according to the flesh, you are about to die." (Rom. 8:13)

35. "I consider that the sufferings of this present time are not worthy to be compared with the glory that is about to be revealed to us." (Rom. 8:18)

36. "It is already the hour for you to awaken from sleep; for now salvation is nearer to us than when we believed. The night is almost gone, and the day is at hand." (Rom. 13:11-12)

37. "The God of peace will soon crush Satan under your feet." (Rom. 16:20)

38. "The time has been shortened." (1 Cor. 7:29)

39. "The form of this world is passing away." (1 Cor. 7:31)

40. "Now these things… were written for our instruction, upon whom the ends of the ages have come." (1 Cor. 10:11)

41. "We shall not all fall sleep, but we shall all be changed, in a moment, in the twinkling of an eye, at the last trumpet; for the trumpet will sound, and the dead will be raised imperishable, and we shall be changed." (1 Cor. 15:51-52)

42. "Maranatha!" [The Lord comes!] (1 Cor. 16:22)

43. "…not only in this age, but also in the one about to come." (Eph. 1:21)

44. "The LORD is near." (Phil. 4:5)

45. "The gospel... was proclaimed in all creation under heaven." (Col. 1:23; compare Matt. 24:14; Rom. 10:18; 16:26; Col. 1:5-6; 2 Tim. 4:17; Rev. 14:6-7; cf. 1 Clement 5, 7)

46. "...things which are a shadow of what is about to come." (Col. 2:16-17)

47. "...we who are alive, and remain until the coming of the LORD... We who are alive and remain shall be caught up together with them in the clouds... You, brethren, are not in darkness, that the Day should overtake you like a thief." (1 Thess. 4:15, 17; 5:4)

48. "May your spirit and soul and body be preserved complete, without blame at the coming of our Lord Jesus Christ." (1 Thess. 5:23)

49. "It is only just for God to repay with affliction those who afflict you, and to give relief to you who are afflicted and to us as well when the Lord Jesus shall be revealed from heaven with His mighty angels in flaming fire." (2 Thess. 1:6-7)

50. "Godliness... holds promise for the present life and that which is about to come." (1 Tim. 4:8)

51. "I charge you... that you keep the commandment without stain or reproach until the appearing of our Lord Jesus Christ." (1 Tim. 6:14)

52. "...storing up for themselves the treasure of a good foundation for that which is about to come, so that they may take hold of that which is life indeed." (1 Tim. 6:19)

53. "In the last days difficult times will come. For men will be lovers of self… Avoid these men. For of these are those who enter into households and captivate weak women… These also oppose the truth… But they will not make further progress; for their folly will be obvious to all…" (2 Tim. 3:1-2, 5-6, 8-9)

54. "I solemnly charge you in the presence of God and of Christ Jesus, who is about to judge the living and the dead…" (2 Tim. 4:1)

55. "God, after He spoke long ago to the fathers in the prophets in many portions and in many ways, in these last days has spoken to us in His Son." (Heb. 1:1-2)

56. "Are they not all ministering spirits, sent out to render service for the sake of those who are about to inherit salvation?" (Heb. 1:14)

57. "He did not subject to angels the world about to come." (Heb. 2:5)

58. "…and have tasted… the powers of the age about to come." (Heb. 6:5)

59. "For ground that drinks the rain which often falls upon it and brings forth vegetation useful to those for whose sake it is also tilled, receives a blessing from God; but if it yields thorns and thistles, it is worthless and near a curse, and it's end is for burning." (Heb. 6:7-8)

60. "When He said, 'A new covenant,' He has made the first obsolete. But whatever is becoming obsolete and growing old is ready to disappear." (Heb. 8:13)

61. "The Holy Spirit is signifying this, that the way of the Holy Places has not yet been revealed, while the outer tabernacle is still standing, which is a symbol for the present time. Accordingly both gifts and sacrifices are offered which cannot make the worshiper perfect in conscience, since they relate only to food and drink and various washings, regulations for the body imposed until a time of reformation." (Heb. 9:8-10; compare Gal. 4:19; Eph. 2:21-22; 3:17; 4:13)

62. "But when Christ appeared as a high priest of the good things about to come..." (Heb. 9:11)

63. "Now once at the consummation of the ages He has been manifested to put away sin." (Heb. 9:26)

64. "For the Law, since it has only a shadow of the good things about to come..." (Heb. 10:1)

65. "...as you see the Day drawing near." (Heb. 10:25)

66. "...the fury of a fire which is about to consume the adversaries." (Heb. 10:27)

67. "For yet in a very little while, He who is coming will come, and will not delay." (Heb. 10:37)

68. "For here we do not have a lasting city, but we are seeking the one that is about to come." (Heb. 13:14)

69. "Speak and so act, as those who are about to be judged by the law of liberty." (James. 2:12)

70. "Come now, you rich, weep and howl for your miseries which are coming upon you… It is in the last days that you have stored up your treasure!" (James. 5:1, 3)

71. "Be patient, therefore, brethren, until the coming of the Lord." (James. 5:7)

72. "You too be patient; strengthen your hearts, for the coming of the Lord is at hand." (James. 5:8)

73. "…salvation ready to be revealed in the last time." (1 Peter 1:5)

74. "He… has appeared in these last times for the sake of you." (1 Peter 1:20)

75. "They shall give account to Him who is ready to judge the living and the dead." (1 Peter 4:5)

76. "The end of all things is at hand; therefore, be of sound judgment and sober spirit for the purpose of prayer." (1 Peter 4:7)

77. "For it is time for judgment to begin with the household of God." (1 Peter 4:17)

78. "…as your fellow elder and witness of the sufferings of Christ, and a partaker also of the glory that is about to be revealed." (1 Peter 5:1)

79. "We have the prophetic word… which you do well to pay attention as to a lamp shining in a dark place, until the Day dawns and the morning star arises in your hearts." (2 Peter 1:19)

80. "Their judgment from long ago is not idle, and their destruction is not asleep." (2 Peter 2:3)

81. "In the last days mockers will come... For this they willingly are ignorant of..." (1 Peter 3:3, 5)

82. "But the day of the LORD will come like a thief, in which the heavens will pass away with a roar and the elements will be destroyed with intense heat, and the earth and its works will be burned up. Since all these things are to be destroyed in this way, what sort of people ought you to be in holy conduct and godliness, looking for and hastening the coming of the day of God." (2 Peter 3:10-12)

83. "The darkness is passing away, and the true light is already shining." (1 Jn. 2:8)

84. "The world is passing away, and its desires." (1 Jn. 2:17)

85. "It is the last hour." (1 Jn. 2:18)

86. "Even now many antichrists have arisen; from this we know that it is the last hour." (1 Jn. 2:18; compare Matt. 24:23-34)

87. "This is that of the antichrist, of which you have heard that it is coming, and now it is already in the world." (1 Jn. 4:3; compare 2 Thess. 2:7)

88. "For certain persons have crept in unnoticed, those who were long beforehand marked out for this condemnation... About these also Enoch... prophesied, saying, 'Behold, the LORD came with many thousands

of His holy ones, to execute judgment upon all, and to convict all the ungodly..." (Jude 1:4, 14-15)

89. "But you, beloved, ought to remember the words that were spoken beforehand by the apostles of our Lord Jesus Christ, that they were saying to you, 'In the last time there shall be mockers, following after their own ungodly lusts.' These are the ones who cause divisions..." (Jude 1:17-19)

90. "...to show to His bond-servants, the things which must shortly take place." (Rev. 1:1)

91. "The time is near." (Rev. 1:3)

92. "Nevertheless what you have, hold fast until I come." (Rev. 2:25)

93. "I also will keep you from the hour of testing which is about to come upon the whole world." (Rev. 3:10)

94. "I am coming quickly." (Rev. 3:11)

95. "And she gave birth to a son, a male child, who is about to rule all the nations with a rod of iron." (Rev. 12:5)

96. "And in her [the Great City Babylon] was found the blood of prophets and of saints and of all who have been slain on the earth." (Rev. 18:24; compare Matt. 23:35-36; Lk. 11:50-51)

97. "...to show to His bond-servants the things which must shortly take place." (Rev. 22:6)

98. "Behold, I am coming quickly." (Rev. 22:7)

99. "Do not seal up the words of the prophecy of this book, for the time is near." (Rev. 22:10; compare Dan. 8:26)

100. "Behold, I am coming quickly." (Rev. 22:12)

101. "Yes, I am coming quickly." (Rev. 22:20)

ENDNOTES

INTRODUCTION

1. Hal Lindsey, *There's A New World Coming*, 1973, pg.15.

CHAPTER 1

1. From an email correspondence, Friday, April 17, 2020.

2. See *5 Notable Failed End Times Prophecies* at: https://www.christianpost.com/news/5-notable-failed-end-times-prophecies-224215/.

3. Ibid.

CHAPTER 2

1. Hal Lindsey, *Countdown to Armageddon*, pgs. 8, 12, 15.

2. Darby. Stow Hill Bible & Tract Depot. Kingston-On-Thames, 1829, *Prophetic No. 1 Vol. 2.*, pgs. 141-160.

3. From the Pro-Crowley website, Lashtal.com: https://www.lashtal.com/forums/topic/john-nelson-darby/.

4. Ibid.

5. Ibid.

6. Ibid.

7. R. T. Magnum and Mark S. Sweetnam, *The Scofield Bible: Its History and Impact on the Evangelical Church*, pp. 188-195.

8. Mr. Grant on "The Darby Brethren" by C.H.Spurgeon, June 1860, Sword and Trowel periodical.

9. Ibid.

CHAPTER 3

1. A.W. Pink, *The Divine Covenants*, Baker Book House, 1973 page 272.

2. Charles Hodge, *Commentary on the Epistle to the Romans*, Wm. B. Eerdmans, 1993, page 305.

3. Quoted from the article, "Not All Of Israel Is Israel" by Greg Bahnsen, https://www.monergism.com/thethreshold/articles/onsite/notallisrael.html.

4. See 1 Samuel 16:7.

5. Matthew Henry, *Commentary on the Whole Bible*, Royal Publishers, 1979, vol. 3, page 456.

6. Matthew Poole, *Commentary on the Whole Bible*, Hendrickson Publishers, vol. 3, pg. 486.

7. Charles C. Ryrie., *Dispensationalism*, pg. 39, 1995 .

8. From Ken Gentry's series of articles, "The Ephesians Road Out Of Dispensationalism", Part 3, "Separating What God Has Joined Together".

9. Ibid.

10. Irenaeus, *Against Heresies*, book 5, chapter 25.

11. Hippolytus, *On Daniel*, II, 39.

12. Owen, John "Complete Works", Vol.17. *Exercitation* 18, p. 560.

13. John Gill, "Exposition of the Old and New Testament, Deuteronomy 30 verse 5.

14. Stephen J. Stein, editor, "Introduction," Jonathan Edwards, Works, *Apocalyptic Writings*, V. 8, pp.17–19.

CHAPTER 4

1. As quoted in Clement of Alexandria's *Miscellanies.*

2. From *Daniel 9:24-27 and the Tribulation,* by LeAnne Snow Flesher, Review and Expositor, 109, Fall 2012.

3. For further study on this concept of the Church as Temple, Priesthood and Sacrifice, read my book *Jesus Unveiled: Forsaking Church As We Know It For Ekklesia As God Intended",* Quoir Publishing, 2019.

4. From *Daniel 9:24-27 and the Tribulation,* by LeAnne Snow Flesher, Review and Expositor, 109, Fall 2012.

5. See my book *Jesus Unbound: Liberating the Word of God from the Bible,* pps 157-178, Quoir Publishing, 2018.

6. Special thanks to author and Bible scholar Steve Gregg for his help answering this question.

7. From a personal email correspondence, April 6, 2020.

CHAPTER 5

1. As quoted in the book *A Short History of the World* by H.G. Wells.

2. See Isaiah 20:1-6 for a description of how Isaiah 19:1 was fulfilled by the Assyrian army.

3. For more examples of God coming in the clouds, see also Psalms 104:1-3; Isaiah 19:1-3; Joel 2:1-2.

4. See *The Annals of Tacitus* for references "commotions" and "disturbances" throughout the Roman Empire in the time leading up to 70 AD.

5. See *Last Days Madness* by Gary Demar, pps. 80-81.

6. Ibid, pg. 79.

7. From the article, *Christian Zionism,* by Dr. Ninan Koshy: https://www.globalministries.org/mee_resources_christian_zionism_koshy.

8. See "The Balfour Declaration: A Scrap of Paper that Changed History" found here: https://fanack.com/palestine/history-past-to-present/balfour-declaration/.

9.   Ibid.

10. As reported in the *New York Times* article, "Trump Recognizes Jerusalem as Israel's Capital and Orders U.S. Embassy to Move" on Dec. 6, 2017.

11. Ibid.

12. For further study, visit the Preterist Archive at: www.preteristarchive. com/StudyArchive/p/pella-flight.html.

CHAPTER 6

1.   Ken Gentry, *Before Jerusalem Fell*, pg.7.

2.   Josephus' account appears in: Cornfield, Gaalya ed., Josephus, *The Jewish War* (1982); Duruy, Victor, History of Rome vol. V (1883).

3.   Philostratus, *The Life of Apollonius of Tyana*.

4.   https://ohr.edu/1088

5.   https://www.chabad.org/library/article_cdo/aid/144575/jewish/What-Is-Tisha-BAv.htm.

6.   http://www.jewfaq.org/holidayd.htm.

7.   Josephus, *Wars of the Jews*, pg. 581-583.

8.   Ibid.

9.   Ibid.

10. Ibid.

11. Ibid.

12. Ibid.

13. Ibid.

14. Ibid.

15. Tacitus, *Historiae V: The Roman Earthworks at Jerusalem*.

CHAPTER 7

1.   Philip Schaff, *History of the Christian Church*, Eerdmans, 1910, pg. 826.

2. For more info, see: http://beyondtheendtimes.com/writing/articles/k_ davies/mark.html.

3. Thanks to the post in the Preterist Archive where this list was found: https://www.preteristarchive.com/2018_drawbaugh_reflections-of-a-former-full-preterist_04/#more-46788.

4. See post on N.T. Wright's website, on July 12, 2016, "Farewell to the Rapture", http://ntwrightpage.com/2016/07/12/farewell-to-the-rapture/.

CHAPTER 8

1. From the introduction to the Book of Revelation, by Brian Zahnd, as published in *The Jesus-Centered Bible*, Group Publishing, 2015.

2. From *Sinners in the Hands of a Loving God* by Brian Zahnd, pp. 152-153

3. From *The Wrath of the Lamb* by Richard Murray, Facebook post, May 29, 2019

4. David Bentley Hart, *The New Testament: A Translation*, notation on Rev. 5:6, pg. 504.

5. From the introduction to the Book of Revelation, by Brian Zahnd, as published in *The Jesus-Centered Bible*, Group Publishing, 2015.

CHAPTER 9

1. From the article "What Would Jesus Do?" by Walter Kirn in *GQ Magazine*, 2003.

2. Ibid.

3. From the Preterist Archive article "The Resurrection of All In All" by Brian Johnson, 2003, https://www.preteristarchive.com/2003_johnson_universalism/.

CHAPTER 10

1. From Arthur Melanson's article "You're A Preterist? What do you have to look forward to?", at the Preterist Archive, 2001 .

APPENDIX A

1. Note: This article was written using various sources of information, most notably from author Steve Gregg https://www.thenarrowpath.com/.

APPENDIX B

1. https://www.bible.ca/archeology/jesus-christ-died-death-cross-eclipse-red-blood-moon-sun-darkness-earthquake-bodies-raised-resurrection-temple-veil-torn-in-two-centurian-son-of-god-3-april-33AD.htm#hagee.

2. http://richardedmondson.net/.

For more information about Keith Giles
or to contact him for speaking engagements,
please visit *www.KeithGiles.com*

Many voices. One message.

Quoir is a boutique publisher
with a singular message: *Christ is all.*
Venture beyond your boundaries to discover Christ
in ways you never thought possible.

For more information, please visit
www.quoir.com

HERETIC HAPPY HOUR

Burning questions, not people.

Heretic Happy Hour is an unapologetically irreverent, crass, and sometimes profound conversation about the Christian faith. Hosts, Keith Giles, Katy Valentine, Derrick Day, and Matthew Distefano pull no punches and leave no stones unturned. For some serious sacred cow-tipping, there's nothing better than spending an hour of your time with us.

www.heretichappyhour.com

CPSIA information can be obtained
at www.ICGtesting.com
Printed in the USA
BVHW060103240820
587115BV00003B/89

9 781938 480652